GOSPEL SHAPED
OUTREACH

Leader's Guide

GOSPEL SHAPED

OUTREACH

Erik Raymond

Gospel Shaped Outreach Leader's Guide
© The Gospel Coalition / The Good Book Company 2015

Published by:
The Good Book Company
Tel (US): 866 244 2165
Tel (UK): 0333 123 0880
Email (US): info@thegoodbook.com
Email (UK): info@thegoodbook.co.uk

Websites:
North America: www.thegoodbook.com
UK: www.thegoodbook.co.uk
Australia: www.thegoodbook.com.au
New Zealand: www.thegoodbook.co.nz

ISBN: 9781909919297 Printed in the US

PRODUCTION TEAM:

AUTHOR:
Erik Raymond

**SERIES EDITOR FOR
THE GOSPEL COALITION:**
Collin Hansen

**SERIES EDITOR FOR
THE GOOD BOOK COMPANY:**
Tim Thornborough

**MAIN TEACHING SESSION
DISCUSSIONS:** Alison Mitchell

DAILY DEVOTIONALS:
Carl Laferton

BIBLE STUDIES:
Tim Thornborough

EDITORIAL ASSISTANTS:
Jeff Robinson (TGC), Rachel Jones (TGBC)

VIDEO EDITOR:
Phil Grout

PROJECT ADMINISTRATOR:
Jackie Moralee

EXECUTIVE PRODUCER:
Brad Byrd

DESIGN:
André Parker

CONTENTS

PREFACE

GROWING A GOSPEL SHAPED CHURCH

The Gospel Coalition is a group of pastors and churches in the Reformed heritage who delight in the truth and power of the gospel, and who want the gospel of Christ crucified and resurrected to lie at the center of all we cherish, preach and teach.

We want churches called into existence by the gospel to be shaped by the gospel in their everyday life.

Through our fellowship, conferences, and online and printed media, we have sought to encourage pastors and church leaders to calibrate their lives around what is of first importance—the gospel of Christ. In these resources, we want to provide those same pastors with the tools to excite and equip church members with this mindset.

In our foundation documents, we identified five areas that should mark the lives of believers in a local fellowship:

1. Empowered corporate worship
2. Evangelistic effectiveness
3. Counter-cultural community
4. The integration of faith and work
5. The doing of justice and mercy

We believe that a church utterly committed to winsome and theologically substantial expository preaching, and that lives out the gospel in these areas, will display its commitment to dynamic evangelism, apologetics, and church planting. These gospel-shaped churches will emphasize repentance, personal renewal, holiness, and the wonderful life of the church as the body of Christ. At the same time, there will be engagement with the social structures of ordinary people, and cultural engagement with art, business, scholarship and government. The church will be characterized by firm devotion to the truth on the one hand, and by transparent compassion on the other.

The Gospel Coalition believes in the priority of the local church, and that the local church is the best place to discuss these five ministry drivers and decide how to integrate them into life and mission. So, while being clear on the biblical principles, these resources give space to consider what a genuine expression of a gospel-shaped church looks like for you in the place where God has put you, and with the people he has gathered into fellowship with you.

Through formal teaching sessions, daily Bible devotionals, group Bible studies and the regular preaching ministry, it is our hope and prayer that congregations will grow into maturity, and so honor and glorify our great God and Savior.

Don Carson
President

Tim Keller
Vice President

INTRODUCTION

Evangelicals, by definition, should believe in and practice evangelism. And yet many churches and Christians can lose sight of this primary goal for our life and work.

This is not an "evangelism course" like many others available. Often these courses will focus on the "how to" of evangelism, offering various techniques, programs and methods of outreach that individuals and churches can use. These can be incredibly helpful in giving us the confidence and skills to explain the good news to others.

But this course is different.

In the nine sessions in this curriculum, I have not sought to show you a particular way of explaining the gospel, but to lay strong biblical foundations for a broad and deep appreciation of the wonderful gospel of grace that we are called to understand, believe, rejoice in and proclaim to a waiting world.

As you work through the material, you will be able to share your own experiences, and benefit from the ideas and encouragement of your fellowship. You will also, no doubt, discover that you need more help and training in specific aspects of your witness for Christ in your community. This course will not be the last word on evangelism, for you or your church. But what I am aiming to do is to impress upon you, both as individuals and as a whole church, a deep conviction that God's mission of salvation in the world is also your mission; and that he is inviting you into the privilege of praying and working to advance his kingdom among your family, friends, neighbors, co-workers and community.

The Gospel Coalition identifies five hallmarks of a gospel-shaped church. One of those is evangelistic effectiveness, about which it says:

> *Because the gospel (unlike religious moralism) produces people who do not disdain those who disagree with them, a truly gospel–centered church should be filled with members who winsomely address people's hopes*

and aspirations with Christ and his saving work. We have a vision for a church that sees conversions of rich and poor, highly educated and less educated, men and women, old and young, married and single, and all races. We hope to draw highly secular and postmodern people, as well as reaching religious and traditional people. Because of the attractiveness of its community and the humility of its people, a gospel–centered church should find people in its midst who are exploring and trying to understand Christianity. It must welcome them in hundreds of ways. It will do little to make them "comfortable" but will do much to make its message understandable. In addition to all this, gospel–centered churches will have a bias toward church planting as one of the most effective means of evangelism there is.

It is my prayer that as you work through this curriculum, you and your church will become more and more the community and people that you are called to be; a fellowship that is effective at, and excited about, bringing the gospel to those around you.

Erik Raymond

MAKING THE MOST OF
GOSPEL SHAPED
CHURCH

WHAT GOSPEL SHAPED CHURCH WILL DO FOR YOU

God is in the business of changing people and changing churches. He always does that through his gospel.

Through the gospel he changed us from his enemies to his friends, and through the gospel he brought us into a new family to care for each other and to do his will in the world. The gospel brings life and creates churches.

But the gospel of Jesus, God's Son, our Savior and Lord, isn't merely what begins our Christian life and forms new churches. It is the pattern, and provides the impetus, for all that follows. So Paul wrote to the Colossian church:

> *Therefore, as you received Christ Jesus the Lord, so walk in him, rooted and built up in him and established in the faith, just as you were taught, abounding in thanksgiving (Colossians 2:6-7).*

Just as you received … so walk… In other words, the secret of growing as a Christian is to continue to reflect upon and build your life on the gospel of the lordship of Jesus Christ. And the secret of growing as a church is to let the gospel inform and energize every single aspect of a church's life, both in what you do and how you do it, from your sermons to young mothers' groups; from your budget decisions and your pastoral care to your buildings maintenance and church bulletins.

Letting the gospel shape a church requires the whole church to be shaped by the gospel. To be, and become, gospel shaped is not a task merely for the senior pastor, or the staff team, or the board of elders. It is something that happens as every member considers the way in which the gospel should continue to shape their walk, and the life of their church.

That is the conviction that lies behind this series of five resources from The Gospel Coalition. It will invite your church members to be part of the way in which you shape your church according to the unchanging gospel, in your particular culture and circumstances. It will excite and equip your whole church to be gospel shaped. It will envision you together, from senior church staff to your newest believer. It will enable you all to own the vision of a gospel-shaped church, striving to teach that gospel to one another and to reach your community with that gospel. As you continue to work out together the implications of the gospel that has saved us, you will be guided into Christian maturity in every area of your lives, both personal and corporate.

This resource is for all kinds of churches: large and small; urban and rural; new plants and long-established congregations; all denominations and none. It is for any congregation that has been given life by the gospel and wants to put the gospel at the center of its life.

You can use the five tracks in any order you like—and you can use as many or as few of them as you wish. If you think your church is lacking in one particular area, it will always be helpful to focus on that for a season. But it is our hope that you will plan to run all five parts of the curriculum with your church—perhaps over a 3- or 4-year time frame. Some tracks may be more like revision and confirmation that you are working well in those areas. Others will open up new areas of service and change that you need to reflect upon. But together they will help you grow into an organic maturity as you reflect on the implications of the gospel in every area of life.

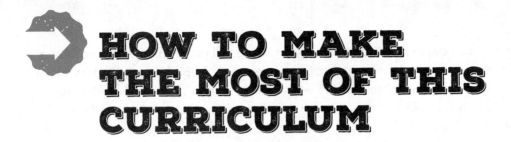

HOW TO MAKE THE MOST OF THIS CURRICULUM

Because the gospel, as it is articulated in the pages of the Bible, should be the foundation of everything we do, this resource is designed to work best if a congregation gives itself over to exploring the themes together as a whole. That means shaping the whole of church life for a season around the theme. The overall aim is to get the DNA of the gospel into the DNA of your church life, structures, practices and people.

So it is vitally important that you involve as many people in your congregation as possible in the process, so that there is a sense that this is a journey that the whole church has embarked upon together. The more you immerse yourselves in this material, the more you will get from it. But equally, all churches are different, and so this material is flexible enough to fit any and every church program and structure—see page 24 for more details.

Here are some other suggestions for how to make the most of this material.

PREPARE

Work through the material in outline with your leadership team and decide which elements best fit where. Will you use the sermon suggestions, or develop a series of your own? Will you teach through the main sessions in Sunday School, or in midweek groups? Will you use the teaching DVD, or give your own talks?

Think about some of the likely pressure points this discussion will create in your congregation. How will you handle in a constructive way any differences of opinion that come out of this? Decide together how you will handle feedback. There will be many opportunities for congregation members to express their ideas and thoughts, and as you invite them to think about your church's life, they will have many suggestions. It will be overwhelming to have everyone emailing or calling the Senior Pastor; but it will be very frustrating if church members feel they are not truly being listened to, and that nothing will really change. So organize a system of feedback from group-discussion leaders and Bible-study leaders; make clear which member of senior staff will collect that feedback; and schedule time as a staff team to listen to your members' thoughts, and pray about and consider them.

There is an online feedback form that could be distributed and used to round off the whole track with your congregation.

PROMOTE

Encourage your congregation to buy into the process by promoting it regularly and building anticipation. Show the trailer at all your church meetings and distribute your own customized version of the bulletin insert (download from www.gospelshapedchurch.org).

Embarking on this course together should be a big deal. Make sure your congregation knows what it might mean for them, and what an opportunity it represents in the life of your whole church; and make sure it sounds like an exciting adventure in faith.

Do involve the whole church. Younger children may not be able to grasp the implications of some things, but certainly those who teach and encourage children of 11 and upwards will be able to adapt the material and outlines here to something that is age appropriate.

PRAY

Pray as a leadership team that the Lord would lead you all into new, exciting ways of serving him.

Encourage the congregation to pray. There are plenty of prompts in the material for this to happen, but do pray at your regular meetings for the Lord's help and guidance as you study, think and discuss together. Building in regular prayer times will help your congregation move together as a fellowship. Prayer connects us to God, but it also connects us to each other, as we address our Father together. And our God "is able to do far more abundantly than all that we ask or think" (Ephesians 3:20-21) as his people ask him to enable them to grasp, and be shaped by, the love of Christ that is shown to us in his gospel.

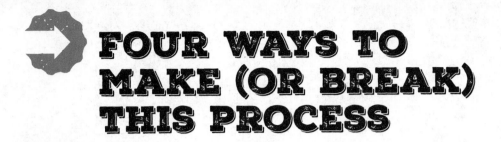

FOUR WAYS TO MAKE (OR BREAK) THIS PROCESS

1. BE OPEN TO CHANGE AS A CHURCH

As churches that love the gospel, we should always be reforming to live more and more in line with that gospel. Change isn't always easy, and is often sacrificial; but it is exciting, and part of the way in which we obey our Lord. Approach this exploration of *Gospel Shaped Outreach* by encouraging your church to be willing to change where needed.

2. BE OPEN TO CHANGE YOURSELF

This curriculum will lead every member to think hard about how the gospel should shape, and in some ways re-shape, your church. You are giving them permission to suggest making changes. As a leader, giving such permission is both exciting and intimidating. It will *make* your course if you enter it as a leadership excited to see how your church may change and how you may be challenged. It will *break* it if you approach it hoping or expecting that your members will simply agree in every way with what you have already decided.

3. DISCUSS GRACIOUSLY

Keep talking about grace and community. Church is about serving others and giving up "my" own wants, not about meeting "my" own social preferences and musical tastes. Encourage your membership to pursue discussions that are positive, open and non-judgmental, and to be able to disagree lovingly and consider other's feelings before their own, rather than seeking always to "win." Model gospel grace in the way you talk about the gospel of grace.

4. REMEMBER WHO IS IN CHARGE

Jesus Christ is Lord of your church—not the leadership, the elders or the membership. So this whole process needs to be bathed in a prayerful sense of commitment to follow him, and to depend on his strength and guidance for any change his Spirit is prompting. Keep reminding your church that this process is not about becoming the church they want, but the one your Lord wants.

HOW TO USE
GOSPEL SHAPED
OUTREACH

HOW TO USE GOSPEL SHAPED OUTREACH

Gospel Shaped Outreach is designed to be a flexible resource to fit a wide variety of church settings. The **Main Teaching Session** is the core of the curriculum—the other components grow out of this. The more elements you use, the greater the benefit will be to your church.

The elements of this course are:

- **MAIN TEACHING SESSION** with DVD or talk, and discussion (core)
- **PERSONAL DEVOTIONALS** (recommended)
- **GROUP BIBLE STUDY** (recommended)
- **PERSONAL JOURNAL** (optional)
- **SERMON SERIES** (suggested passages given)

Each church member will need a copy of the *Gospel Shaped Outreach Handbook*. This contains everything they need to take part in the course, including the discussion questions for the **Main Teaching Session**, **Personal Devotionals**, and the **Group Bible Study**. There's also space to make notes during the sermon, and a **Personal Journal** to keep a record of the things they have been learning.

Each person who will be leading a group discussion, either in the **Main Teaching Session** or the **Group Bible Study**, will need a copy of the *Gospel Shaped Outreach Leader's Guide*. This includes leader's notes to help them guide a small group through the discussion or Bible-study questions, and other resources to give more background and detail. In the Leader's Guide, all the instructions, questions, comments, prayer points etc. that also appear in the Handbook are in **bold text**.

 Further copies of the *Handbook* and *Leader's Guide* are available from
WWW.GOSPELSHAPEDCHURCH.ORG/OUTREACH

A FLEXIBLE CURRICULUM

Gospel Shaped Outreach is designed to be a flexible resource. You may be able to give your whole church over to working through it. If so, a typical week might look like this:

SUNDAY

- Adult Sunday school: **Main Teaching Session** using DVD or live talk (talk outline given in **Leader's Guide**)
- Morning service: **Sermon** based on main theme (suggested Bible passages given in the **Leader's Guide**)

MIDWEEK

- Small groups work through the **Group Bible Study**

CHURCH MEMBERS

- Use the **Personal Devotionals** from Monday to Saturday
- Use the **Personal Journal** to record their thoughts, questions and ideas about things they've been learning throughout the week

Or, if you choose to use the curriculum on a midweek basis, it may be like this:

MIDWEEK

- Small groups work through the **Main Teaching Session** using the DVD

CHURCH MEMBERS

- Use the **Personal Devotionals** from Monday to Saturday
- Use the **Personal Journal** to record their thoughts, questions and ideas about things they've been learning throughout the week

Or you can use the components in any other way that suits your church practice.

HOW TO USE EACH ELEMENT

These sample pages from the *Gospel Shaped Outreach Handbook* show the different elements of the curriculum.

All of the material in this curriculum quotes from and is based on the ESV Bible.

MAIN TEACHING SESSION

- 60 minutes
- Choose between DVD or live talk
- Discussion questions to help group members discuss the DVD/talk and apply it to their own lives and their church
- Guidance for answering the questions is given in the *Leader's Guide*
- Suggestions for praying together

This is the core of the curriculum. It can be run using the *Gospel Shaped Outreach DVD*, or by giving a live talk. A summary of the talk is included in the *Leader's Guide* (see page 34 for an example). A full editable script can also be downloaded from **www.gospelshapedchurch.org/outreach/talks**.

In each session, the DVD/talk is split into either two or three sections, each followed by some discussion questions. At the end of the session there are suggestions to help the group pray specifically for each other.

The discussion questions are designed to help church members unpack the teaching they have heard and apply it to their own lives and to the church as a whole. There are not necessarily right and wrong answers to some of the questions, as this will often depend on the context of your own church. Let group members discuss these openly, and apply them to their own situation.

Keep the discussion groups the same each week if possible, with the same leader (who will need a copy of this *Leader's Guide*) for each group, so that relationships are deepened and the discussions can build on those of previous sessions.

PERSONAL DEVOTIONALS

- Six devotionals with each session
- Designed to be started the day after the main teaching session
- Linked with the theme for each teaching session, but based on different Bible passages
- Help church members dig more deeply into the theme on a daily basis

Each session is followed by six personal devotionals that build on the main theme. They are ideal for church members to use between sessions. For example, if you have the main teaching session on a Sunday, church members can then use the devotionals from Monday to Saturday.

These short devotionals can be used in addition to any regular personal Bible study being done by church members. They would also form a useful introduction for anyone trying out personal Bible reading for the first time.

As well as being in the group member's *Handbook*, the personal devotionals are available for a small fee on the Explore Bible Devotional app. This can be downloaded from the iTunes App Store or Google Play (search for "Explore Bible Devotional"). Select "Gospel Shaped Outreach" from the app's download menu.

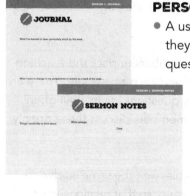

PERSONAL JOURNAL

- A useful place for church members to note down what they have been learning throughout the week, and any questions they may have.

SERMON NOTES

- If the Sunday sermon series is running as part of *Gospel Shaped Outreach*, this is a helpful place to make notes.

GROUP BIBLE STUDY

- 40 – 50 minutes
- An ideal way for small groups to build on what they have been learning in the main teaching
- Uses a different Bible passage from the DVD/talk
- Suggested answers to the questions are given in the *Leader's Guide*

This study is ideal for a home group or other group to work through together. It builds on the theme covered by the main teaching session, but is based on a different Bible passage. You can see the passages and themes listed in the grid on pages 28-29.

If possible, give 40 – 50 minutes for the Bible study. However, it can be covered in 30 minutes if necessary, and if you keep a close eye on time. If your church is not using the Bible studies as part of a regular group, they would also be suitable for individuals to do on their own or in a pair if they want to do some further study on the themes being looked at in the course.

SERMON SUGGESTIONS

The *Leader's Guide* gives a choice of three sermon suggestions to tie in with each session:

- A passage that is used in the main teaching session (DVD or live talk).
- The Bible reading that is being studied in the Group Bible Study that week.
- A third passage that is not being used elsewhere, but that picks up on the same themes. This is the passage that is listed in the overview grid on pages 28-29.

FURTHER READING

At the end of each session in the *Leader's Guide* you will find a page of suggestions for further reading. This gives ideas for books, articles, blog posts, videos, etc. that relate to the session, together with some quotes that you might use in sermons, discussion groups and conversations. Some of these may be helpful in your preparation, as well as helping any group members who want to think more deeply about the topic they've been discussing.

CURRICULUM OUTLINE AT A GLANCE

SESSION	MAIN TEACHING (DVD/TALK)	PERSONAL DEVOTIONS	GROUP BIBLE STUDY	SERMON*
1 How are we doing?	The priority of outreach for both the local church and individual Christians. Various passages including **Romans 10:13-15** and **Ephesians 6:18-20**.	Looking at Paul's trip to Athens in **Acts 17**, seeing what we can learn about our evangelism from the apostle's example.	**Acts 1:1-11** Helping group members see the priority of outreach clearly, and assess where they are at in their own thinking, and in the thinking of the whole church.	ROM 1:13-17
2 Who is Jesus?	Unpacking core truths about Jesus Christ. Various passages including **Luke 9:22, 1 Peter 3:18, John 1:3** and **Matthew 28:18-20**.	Looking into aspects of Jesus' identity that were highlighted in the main teaching session—taken from the **Gospel of Matthew**.	**Colossians 1:15-23** Reinforcing core truths about Christ that show how amazing the Lord Jesus really is—and what a privilege it is that we get to tell the world about him.	REV 1:9-19
3 Who are we?	Establishing our identity as missionaries. Based on **Matthew 28:18-20** and **John 14:15; 20:21**.	**1 Peter 2**, showing us the church's identity and how declaring God's excellence to the world is at the heart of God's purpose for his church.	**Acts 2:42-47; 4:18-31** We are part of a family on a mission. Our lives, both as individuals and as a group, should be focused on that mission.	2 KINGS 7:3-16
4 Who are we reaching?	How should we view unbelievers? Various passages including **Matthew 9:35-38**.	The compassion of the Lord Jesus, seen in how he interacted with a variety of hungry, hurting people in **Mark, Luke** and **John**.	**Ephesians 2:1-10** How does God see unbelievers? How can we more constructively communicate with them the liberating gospel of grace?	GEN 3:1-24
5 What is the gospel plan?	The gospel was God's plan from the very beginning. Based on **Genesis 3,11 and 12, Revelation 5** and **Matthew 28**.	Episodes from the lives of **Abraham, Moses, Naaman, David** and **Esther**, showing how God pointed forward to the life, death, resurrection and rule of his Son, Jesus.	**Acts 16:11-34** Helping group members to be clear about God's part and our part in evangelism, and to see how God's gospel is for everyone.	ACTS 13:13-43

SESSION	MAIN TEACHING (DVD/TALK)	PERSONAL DEVOTIONS	GROUP BIBLE STUDY	SERMON*
6 How should we pray?	Encouraging us to pray for workers, opportunities, boldness, clarity and blessing. Based on **Matthew 9:35-38**, **Colossians 4:2-4** and **Ephesians 6:18-20**.	Colossians 4:2-6, seeing how Paul emphasizes the need for our prayers, our words and our lifestyles each to be committed to sharing the gospel.	**1 Timothy 2:1-7** When we pray for our evangelism, we are praying within the will of God; we are asking him to do the very thing he has told and shown us he wants to do in the world.	MATT 6:7-15
7 What do we say?	Our message must be focused on speaking about Jesus. Based on **1 Corinthians 15:1-8**.	Six instances of communicating the gospel in the **Gospels** and the book of **Acts**.	**Acts 10:1-3; 34-44** How to express essential gospel truths in ways that are relevant and understandable in our culture.	ROM 3:21-26
8 How do we speak?	How do we talk with others about the gospel? How can we live in ways that grow our opportunities for reaching out to others? **1 Corinthians 3:6-7**	**1 Peter 3:14-18**, focusing on the context for our witnessing in a world that rejects Christ; and the heart, words and manner of the gospel witness.	**John 4:1-30** Looking at one way the Lord Jesus modeled evangelism, and thinking about specific ways we can live as "people on mission."	1 THESS 2:2-12
9 How do we keep going?	How can we ensure that evangelism remains at the heart of church life? Various passages including **1 Corinthians 15:3, Ephesians 4:11-15** and **Matthew 28:19-20**.	In **Matthew 9:35 – 10:8**, we see Jesus' compassion for the lost; his prayer for workers; his call to his people to go and proclaim his kingdom; and his training for the mission field.	**2 Corinthians 5:11-20** Tying together everything we've been thinking about by looking at the motivation for evangelism, and what a privilege it is to be part of God's mission in the world.	2 COR 4:1-18

* **NOTE:** The *Leader's Guide* gives three sermon suggestions to tie in with each session. The first picks up a passage from the Main Teaching Session; the second uses the passage from the Group Bible Study; and the third is a new passage, linked with the theme but not used elsewhere in the session. This third passage is the one listed here.

 DOWNLOADS

In addition to the material in this *Leader's Guide,* there are a number of extra downloadable resources and enhancements. You will find all of them listed under the Outreach track at **www.gospelshapedchurch.org** and on The Good Book Company's website: **www.thegoodbook.com**.

- **DIGITAL DOWNLOAD OF DVD MATERIAL.** If you have already bought a DVD as part of the *Leader's Kit*, you will have access to a single HD download of the material using the code on the download card. If you want to download additional digital copies, in SD or HD, these can be purchased from The Good Book Company website: **www.thegoodbook.com/gsc**.

- **DVD TRAILERS.** Trailers and promotional pieces for the series as a whole and for the individual tracks can be downloaded for free. Use these trailers to excite your church about being involved in *Gospel Shaped Church*.

- **TALK OUTLINES.** We're conscious that for some churches and situations, it may be better to deliver your own talk for the main session so that it can be tailored specifically to your people and context. You can download the talk transcript as both a PDF and as an editable Word document.

- **FEEDBACK FORMS.** Because *Gospel Shaped Church* is designed as a whole-church exploration, it's important that you think through carefully how you will handle suggestions and feedback. There's some guidance for that on pages 17-18. We've provided a downloadable feedback form that you can use as part of the way in which you round off your time using the resource. Simply print it and distribute it to your church membership to gather their thoughts and ideas, and to get a sense of the issues you may want to focus on for the future. In addition, there are also fully editable versions of this feedback form so that you can create your own customized sheet that works effectively for the way in which you have used this material, and which suits your church membership. Alternatively, you could use the questions to create your own online feedback form with Google Forms or some other software, to make collecting and collating information easier.

- **RESOURCE LIST.** For each session in this *Leader's Guide* we have included a list of resources that will help you in your preparation for sermons, discussions, Bible studies and other conversations. On the *Gospel Shaped Church* website, you will find an up-to-date list of resources, plus a shorter downloadable list that you might consider giving to church members to supplement their own reading and thinking.

- **BULLETIN TEMPLATES.** Enclosed with the *Leader's Kit* is a sample of a bulletin-insert design to promote the Outreach track to your church. You can download a printable PDF of the design from the *Gospel Shaped Church* website to add your own details, and to print and distribute to your congregation.

- **OTHER PROMOTIONAL MATERIAL.** Editable powerpoint slides and other promotional material to use.

 WWW.GOSPELSHAPEDCHURCH.ORG/OUTREACH

 WWW.THEGOODBOOK.COM/GSC/OUTREACH

SESSION 1:

HOW ARE WE DOING?

WHAT IS GOSPEL-SHAPED EVANGELISM, AND HOW SHOULD
THAT MOLD OUR CHURCH? THESE ARE THE QUESTIONS
WE WILL BE CONSIDERING IN THESE SESSIONS. FIRST,
WE NEED TO SEE WHAT EVANGELISM ACTUALLY IS; THEN
UNDERSTAND WHAT AN EVANGELISTIC CHURCH CULTURE
WOULD LOOK LIKE; AND FINALLY REFLECT UPON WHERE
WE ARE AT IN OUR OWN CHURCH AND LIVES.

TALK OUTLINE

1.1 • Over the next nine sessions, we're going to work out how we can encourage each other to share the good news. So we begin with a simple question:

- ### WHAT IS EVANGELISM?
  Evangelism is the action of telling people the gospel. Evangelism can feel difficult but it's every Christian's responsibility.
  - Matthew 28:19 reminds us the tone of the New Testament is evangelistic.
  - Romans 10:14: For someone to become a disciple, a messenger is required.
  - Matthew 28:20: Jesus commanded all his disciples to be active in evangelism.

- ### WHERE ARE WE AT WITH EVANGELISM?
  Most of us know we're responsible for evangelism, but we're just not doing it. We need to become or grow in being a church with a culture of faithful evangelism. What does this look like in practice?

1.2 • **PRAY FOR OPPORTUNITIES** *Ephesians 6:18-20*
  - We need divine help to overcome our personal weakness.
  - Evangelism is not only the work of people; it is also the work of God.
  - Paul prays for faithfulness as well as fearlessness.

- **TAKE OPPORTUNITIES** *Acts 16:25-34*
  Paul doesn't take the opportunity to escape from prison; he sees and takes the opportunity to share the gospel.

- **MAKE OPPORTUNITIES** *Acts 17:16-17*
  - Evangelism should be motivated by a jealousy for God's glory, as well as compassion for others.
  - A lack of evangelism must mean we are being selfish.

- **CONCLUSION:** We must all be part of cultivating a culture of evangelistic faithfulness by praying for, making, and taking opportunities for the gospel.

 You can download a full transcript of these talks at
WWW.GOSPELSHAPEDCHURCH.ORG/OUTREACH/TALKS

HOW ARE WE DOING?

* Ask the group members to turn to Session 1 on page 13 of the Handbook.

Discuss

What comes into your mind when you hear the word "evangelism?"

This starter question is to get people thinking and talking about their own experience of telling others about Jesus or attending evangelistic events. Some people will be excited. Others will be nervous or feel guilty. Some may talk about embarrassment at terrible evangelistic events they've been to, or conversations they've had. There is no wrong answer to this question—the aim is just to get people talking.

It's also an opportunity to clarify any misunderstandings people may have about what "evangelism" means. Some in your group may be confused about the difference between "evangelism," "evangelical" and "evangelistic."

In this course, we will define evangelism as "the action of telling people the gospel."

▶ **WATCH DVD 1.1** (6 min 31 sec) **OR DELIVER TALK 1.1** (see page 34)

* Encourage the group to make notes as they watch the DVD or listen to the talk. There is space for notes on page 15 of the Handbook.

Discuss

**"Over time, evangelism becomes less of a reflex and more of a challenge."
Do you agree? Have you experienced a gradual decline in your own personal
evangelism? What factors do you think might have contributed to this?**

This question gives the group an opportunity to begin to think about their
own experience of sharing the gospel with others. Encourage people to be
honest. Factors may include fear of how people will respond, living a busy life,
feeling indifferent, not knowing what to say, or not believing that telling others
will make any difference. They may feel guilty about their lack of evangelism.
Encourage them that this course aims to help everyone be excited about
sharing the good news about Jesus, and able to make and take opportunities
to do this.

 **ROMANS 10:13-15**

¹³ *For "everyone who calls on the name of the Lord will be saved."*
¹⁴ *How then will they call on him in whom they have not believed? And how
are they to believe in him of whom they have never heard? And how are
they to hear without someone preaching?* ¹⁵ *And how are they to preach
unless they are sent? As it is written, "How beautiful are the feet of those
who preach the good news!"*

**What needs to happen before someone becomes a Christian ("calls on the
name of the Lord")? List the steps from the passage.**

These verses show what is necessary for someone to "[call] on the name of the
Lord" (v 13)—which means (v 9) to call Jesus Lord and believe in him.
- In order to call, they need to believe in him (v 14).
- In order to believe in him, they need to have heard (v 14).
- In order to hear, someone needs to tell them (v 14).

NOTE: Explain that the word "preaching" (v 14) does not mean to stand in a
pulpit and deliver a sermon. It is a general word that simply means "proclaim"
or "tell" the good news about Jesus. When you are talking conversationally
about Jesus to someone over a cup of coffee, you are "preaching" to them.

In verse 15, Paul describes evangelism as "beautiful." Why do we often forget that evangelism is like this?

You may want to refer back to the opening question on page 15 of the Handbook. It's unlikely that anyone gave "beautiful" as their answer. Why is that? It may be that many in your group see evangelism as a chore they "ought" to do, rather than seeing it as Paul sees it: something delightful that is a joy and privilege to be involved in.

▶ **WATCH DVD 1.2** (5 min 4 sec) **OR DELIVER TALK 1.2** (see page 34)

* *Encourage the group to make notes as they watch the DVD or listen to the talk. There is space for notes on page 16 of the Handbook.*

Discuss

👉 **EPHESIANS 6:18-20**

> [18] *To that end keep alert with all perseverance, making supplication for all the saints,* [19] *and also for me, that words may be given to me in opening my mouth boldly to proclaim the mystery of the gospel,* [20] *for which I am an ambassador in chains, that I may declare it boldly, as I ought to speak.*

1. PRAY

Why do you think Paul asks them to pray for "words" and for boldness?

Most people struggle in evangelism for two reasons. We worry that we are going to say the wrong thing or won't know what to say. And we are fearful of how people will react—which often means we don't say anything at all. It's really encouraging to see that these were precisely the things that Paul needed prayer for. Notice that he asks for boldness twice!

When was the last time you asked someone to pray for your faithfulness in evangelism?

Don't worry if no one in the group has done this—just move on to the next question.

Think of someone you can ask to pray for you and your faithfulness to "declare it boldly."

Encourage group members to write down the name of at least one person. This makes it far more likely that they will follow it up.

2. TAKE

When Paul and Silas were in prison, the earthquake gave them the opportunity to escape—but they didn't. Instead, they took the opportunity to tell their jailer the gospel (Acts 16:23-34).

Honestly, what do you think your response would have been if you had been Paul or Silas? Would you have taken the opportunity to escape?

Encourage honest answers, but don't spend too long on this question.

Can you recall an example when God gave you an evangelistic opportunity in a surprising way? Did you take it? If not, what stopped you?

If you are met with silence, be prepared to give an example from your own experience if you can. Ask why we often choose a life of ease rather than a life of evangelism. What do we miss out on as a result?

3. MAKE

"The only qualification for evangelism is to be a Christian." Does this surprise you? How is it an exciting challenge?

It's easy to think only clergy, church leaders and full-time evangelists have the skills (and responsibility) for evangelism. But every Christian knows and has personally experienced the truth of the gospel. We all have good news to share! It's exciting because we all *can* do it. It's challenging because we all *should*.

What did you hear on the DVD / in the talk that particularly motivated you to tell people the gospel message?

You may want to make a note of these to refer back to in future sessions.

Think of two people you would like to share the gospel with in the next month. Discuss how you could make opportunities to do this. Commit to praying regularly for one another, and to asking each other how this is going.

Encourage your group to choose two people each and write down their names in their Handbooks. You may want to pair up group members so that they pray for each other and hold each other accountable (eg: asking regularly how things are going, and encouraging their partner to make and take opportunities with the people they have listed).

Pray

Pray for your church as it works through this curriculum. Pray that you will grow in your excitement about the gospel, that you will encourage one another, and that you will learn together what it means to be a church that has a culture of evangelism.

Pray for each other individually that you will make opportunities to share the gospel with the two people you listed above, and that you will have the words to say and the boldness to say them.

Pray that you will share the Lord's compassion for those who are hopeless and helpless without Jesus; and that you will be jealous for God's glory.

DAILY BIBLE DEVOTIONALS

As you finish the session, point group members to the daily devotionals to do at home over the course of the next week. There are six of them, beginning on page 20, and followed by a page for journaling. This week the devotionals walk through Acts 17 and Paul's trip to Athens, seeing what we can learn about our evangelism from the apostle's example.

SERMONS

OPTION ONE: MATTHEW 28:16-20

This is a passage Erik focuses on in his DVD presentation, which could be expanded on in a longer sermon.

OPTION TWO: ACTS 1:1-11

This is the passage the Bible study is based on (see next page), which could also be expanded upon in a sermon.

OPTION THREE: ROMANS 1:13-17

This passage is not mentioned in this material, but picks up on several of the themes of this session, especially:
- The obligation (or debt) of God's people to give the gospel to all we meet (v 14).
- The challenge to God's people to be eager about, not ashamed of, proclaiming the gospel (v 15-16).
- The power of God in the gospel—it is the way he saves all kinds of people, by revealing the way in which he makes sinners righteous (v 16-17).

If one of your Sunday sermons is to be based on the theme of this session, church members will find a page to write notes on the sermon on page 27 of their Handbooks.

BIBLE STUDY

AIM: The main teaching session for this week focuses on establishing the priority of outreach for the mission of both the local church and individual Christians. This Bible study on the opening verses of Acts will help group members to see this priority clearly, and assess where they are at with outreach in their own thinking, and in the thinking of the whole church.

Discuss

Many businesses list their main aims as a "mission statement" to help them keep focused when making decisions, and to order their priorities.

Talk about some of these that you know—perhaps a company that you have worked for. What happens when an organization does not have specific aims or priorities?

Outreach, discipleship and evangelism should be the very highest priority for the local church. This opening discussion gets people thinking about how important it is for organizations in general to be clear about very specific aims for their organizations. When they are unclear, or unexpressed, organizations quickly lose their way and chase after all kinds of fads and false ideas. When an organization has a decision to make, it can easily be tested against the mission statement.

> **OPTIONAL:** Write out these famous mission statements on index cards and ask people to guess which company they belong to. You could go on to ask if they are "good" mission statements. Has the company kept to them in your opinion?
>
> *"We create happiness by providing the finest in entertainment for people of all ages, everywhere."* Disney
>
> *"To build a place where people can come to find and discover anything they might want to buy online."* Amazon

"To Refresh the World... in body, mind, and spirit. To inspire moments of optimism and happiness... To Create Value and Make a Difference... " Coca Cola

"We sell high quality food and beverage products." Pepsi

"To bring inspiration and innovation to every athlete in the world. (If you have a body, you are an athlete.)" Nike

"We believe, very simply, that it is the actions of individuals working together that build strong communities ... and that business has an obligation to support those actions in the communities it serves." Bank of America

"We save people money so they can live better." Wal Mart

"To make the world's information universally accessible and useful." Google

OPTIONAL: If your church has one, you might also want to include your own mission statement. Do people know it? Do they think their church is recognizable from it?

👉 READ ACTS 1:1-11

¹ In the first book, O Theophilus, I have dealt with all that Jesus began to do and teach...

1. What is exciting about the word "began" in Acts 1:1?

Jesus has ascended (v 9) and now reigns in heaven. But his work has not stopped. He continues to work in the world through his people, by the power of the Holy Spirit. "The Acts of the Apostles" might also be named "The Acts of Jesus by his Holy Spirit, through the Lives of the Apostles."

2. What does Jesus want the disciples to do, and why (v 4-8)? Why might they have felt terrified by this command?

Jesus wants them to:
- stay in Jerusalem and wait for the gift of the Holy Spirit (v 4).
- be his witnesses in Jerusalem, but then to Judea, Samaria and the whole world (v 8).

The disciples may have been fearful because Jerusalem was the city where Jesus had been killed. The size of the task that Jesus gives to them is enormous. Many of them were not educated men. They may have felt that they were not up to the task, and lacked the skill, motivation and power.

3. **What are the suggestions in the passage that Jesus' plans for his people are different from what the disciples expected (v 6-8)?**

The disciples still appeared to think that the kingdom of Jesus would be a physical rule in Israel (v 6). They had not yet understood that the kingdom of Christ would be "spiritual," rather than physical, until Jesus returns. The implication here is that this is a gospel that spreads through a message and not by political power or conquest.

4. **Jesus speaks of witnesses going "to the end of the earth" (v 8). How does this show that he had in mind not only those he was speaking to, but all his followers, throughout the ages?**

There is no way that those few apostles could take this message to the ends of the earth. It quickly becomes apparent in Acts that the message is spread by other leaders (eg: Stephen, Philip, Barnabas, etc.) as well as the many ordinary believers who spread initially from persecution (see Acts 11:19-21 for example). Additionally, the empowering Holy Spirit came upon all the believers at Pentecost and subsequently, not just to the apostles.

5. **What did the first disciples need in order to be able to spread the gospel (see verses 2, 3, 5, 8)? What would go wrong if one of these was missing?**

- Instruction from Jesus (v 2). They needed to know how to live as disciples.
- Evidence (v 3). They were to be witnesses to his life, death and resurrection. They did this on the basis of solid evidence that Jesus provided for them.
- Power (v 5). The gift of the Holy Spirit to enable them to speak the truth with boldness in the face of hostility and opposition.
- The command (v 8). The very specific command to share the gospel with the whole world—their kinfolk, their enemies (Samaria) and even those they thought were outside the purposes of God.

Without acting like Jesus, by following instruction from Jesus, we are all about the message, without a godly life to adorn the gospel. Without the evidence, the gospel is just our opinion, or a feeling we have. Without power, we would fail. Without the specifics of the command, we would only do it when we felt like it, or limit the scope of the gospel by only sharing it with people we thought deserved it or were open to it.

Do we need anything different?

No. The only difference is that we rely on the evidence of Jesus' life, death and resurrection as provided by the apostolic witness in the Bible.

6. So how does Jesus work in the world today to spread the gospel?

He works by his Holy Spirit through the words and witness of his people.

7. What is the implication of what the angels say in v 11? What were the apostles still hanging onto, and what should they have been doing? How can we be similarly confused?

They needed to get on with it. The experience of the physical presence of Jesus with them was over when he ascended into heaven. Not unnaturally, they still longed for his presence, and were wanting him to return; but their instructions now were simple. *Go to Jerusalem; wait until you receive the gift of the Spirit; then spread the good news to the ends of the earth, until he comes again.*

The implication for us is clear—we are still part of the same timeline. We must be his witnesses to the ends of the earth until he returns. Staring up into heaven may feel "spiritual" but it is not what we are here for!

Acts plays out this pattern as Jesus' promise is fulfilled when the Holy Spirit is given on the day of Pentecost. What is the first thing that Peter does (see 2:14)? He preaches the good news about Jesus.

Apply

FOR YOURSELF: Where would you list "telling the good news about Jesus to others" on the list of your personal priorities? What do you struggle with most—the desire to witness, the words to say, or the boldness to say them?

Encourage people to think about this and share their answers.

FOR YOUR CHURCH: Look over your church calendar of events. What do you conclude about how important outreach is to you as a church family at the moment? Are you praying for, taking and making opportunities to share the gospel as a church together?

It is really important that this discussion does not become an opportunity for blaming others or criticizing the church leadership. Emphasize that this curriculum is a journey we are sharing together—we want to grow together in obedience to Christ, and encourage each other to please our Savior as a body of his followers. As a small-group leader, think about how you can take any suggestions and thoughts generated by this discussion, and communicate them helpfully and constructively to your church leadership.

Be careful also to manage any expectations of rapid change. Sometimes things can change quickly. But often things take shape gradually.

Pray

FOR THE GROUP: Ask God to give you opportunities, the words and boldness to speak about the gospel of Christ.

FOR YOUR WHOLE CHURCH: Pray that working through this curriculum would be a constructive exercise for your church. Pray for unity and for your leaders. And pray that the end result will be that your church is more committed to gospel-shaped outreach.

FURTHER READING

> *It's no accident that you know the people you do. It's no accident that they're in your path. They need the gospel. You know the gospel. God wants them to hear the gospel.*
> **Rico Tice**

> *It is the duty of every Christian to be Christ to his neighbor.*
> **Martin Luther**

> *The Great Commission is not an option to be considered; it is a command to be obeyed.*
> **J. Hudson Taylor**

Books

- *The Gospel and Personal Evangelism (Mark Dever)*
- *Honest Evangelism (Rico Tice)*
- *Evangelism and the Sovereignty of God (J.I. Packer)*
- *Simple Church (Thom Rainer & Eric Geiger)*
- *The Gospel: How the Church Portrays the Beauty of Christ (Ray Ortlund)*

Online

- *Seven Things I'm Learning About Evangelism: gospelshapedchurch.org/resource211*

LEADER'S REFLECTIONS

SESSION 2:
WHO IS JESUS?

WE'VE SEEN THAT EVANGELISM IS THE ACTION OF
TELLING PEOPLE THE GOSPEL; AND THAT AS A CHURCH
WE NEED TO BE COMMITTED TO PRAYING FOR, MAKING,
AND TAKING OPPORTUNITIES TO TALK ABOUT THE
GOSPEL MESSAGE. THAT MESSAGE CENTERS ON JESUS.
BUT... JUST WHO *IS* JESUS?
IN THIS SESSION, WE'LL CONSIDER WHAT ASPECTS
OF HIS IDENTITY WE NEED TO UNDERSTAND AND BE
EXCITED BY, SO THAT WE'LL BE ABLE AND WILLING TO
TELL OTHERS WHAT THEY NEED TO HEAR.

TALK OUTLINE

2.1 ● Jesus seems to be everywhere in popular culture—but there's confusion over who he really is. So who is Jesus?

- **HE IS GOD IN THE FLESH**
  Jesus is 100% God and 100% man.
  - John 8:58: Jesus did not have a beginning.
  - John 1:1-3: It was through Jesus that God created the world.
  - Colossians 2:9: Jesus is God in the flesh.

2.2 ● **HE IS THE RESURRECTED KING**
  - The New Testament is full of references to the resurrection: eg: 1 Corinthians 15:12, 20; Revelation 1:5; 1 Peter 1:3-4
  - Matthew 28:18-20: The gospel message is: "Jesus is Lord."

- **HE IS THE TRUTH-TELLING LORD** *Luke 9:22; John 10:17-18*
  Jesus accurately predicted his own death and resurrection. He did things only God can do, so his words are trustworthy and powerful.

- **HE IS THE SIN-BEARING SAVIOR** *1 Peter 3:18*
  Our sin separates us from God. What are the options for reconciliation?
  1. God can compromise and forgive everyone. This is a false hope.
  2. We can try to make up for our sins. This is a false hope.
  3. Jesus can step in for us and take our place. This is the only real hope.

- **HE IS THE ONLY WAY TO GOD** *Acts 4:12; John 14:6; John 3:36; 1 Timothy 2:5*
  It's unfashionable to speak of the exclusivity of Jesus, but God's word is clear: Jesus is the only way to God.

- **CONCLUSION:** We don't have to get people talking about Jesus—he is everywhere. But we do have to be sure we are talking about the real Jesus.

 You can download a full transcript of these talks at
WWW.GOSPELSHAPEDCHURCH.ORG/OUTREACH/TALKS

WHO IS JESUS?

- *Ask the group members to turn to Session 2 on page 29 of the Handbook.*

Discuss

If you asked a random set of people at your local shopping mall who they thought Jesus was or is, what different answers would you get?

This question is designed to be a simple introduction to the subject, and to help group members think about the views of Jesus that non-Christians may have.

Which of these views do you think is growing in popularity?

There's no wrong answer to this question. It may depend on the kind of area you live in. It will help the group start to think about which views are common now, rather than when they first became Christians. Believers can easily get disconnected from the culture in general, or local culture in particular, and not be up to date with what people are thinking, and therefore with how to engage with them with the gospel. This discussion may reveal areas of concern for you as a leader.

▶ **WATCH DVD 2.1** (4 min 25 sec) **OR DELIVER TALK 2.1** (see page 50)

- *Encourage the group to make notes as they watch the DVD or listen to the talk. There is space for notes on page 31 of the Handbook.*

Discuss

The Bible reveals to us that God is a Trinity—a Tri (three) Unity—Father, Son and Holy Spirit.

Is the Trinity a subject you would bring up in an evangelistic conversation? Why or why not?

Group members may vary in how confident they feel in their own understanding of the Trinity. None of us will fully understand the joy and complexity of how God can be three in one until we see him face to face in the new creation. But this isn't an excuse not to talk to non-Christians about it!

The gospel message is the good news about *Jesus Christ*. That's why this session is all about Jesus. Steering an evangelistic conversation to be about Jesus is a helpful way to focus on the uniqueness of the Christian gospel; and asking a non-Christian who they think Jesus is quickly shows their understanding of the biblical Jesus. So, for many group members, this is going to be a good starting point.

However, some non-Christians will raise the subject of the Trinity themselves. We shouldn't be afraid of telling them what the Bible says about God—that he is Trinity—three distinct, co-existent Persons; co-equal Persons; co-eternal Persons. The Bible does not use the term "Trinity" when referring to God, but it does show clearly that he is trinitarian. For example, at the baptism of Jesus (Mark 1 v 9-11), where God the Son is baptized, God the Holy Spirit descends on him like a dove, and God the Father declares his pleasure in his Son. The good news is that the doctrine of the Trinity shows us that at the heart of the universe there is a relationship of love.

"Jesus is fully God—100%—and wholly man—100%." Which of these do you find hardest to grasp? Why is it vital for the gospel message that both of these things are true?

Different members of your group will answer the first part of this question differently; but most of us, if not all, struggle at times to remember the God-ness of this human, Jesus of Nazareth; or the humanity of God the Son, Jesus of Nazareth.

If Jesus were not God, he would not be able authoritatively to teach us about God and eternity; he would not be worthy of the worship he receives and accepts in the Gospels; he would need to die for his own sinful nature, and so could not die for ours; and he would not be able to rule us perfectly.

If Jesus were not really a man, he would not be able to represent us; he would not be able to obey for us, in our place, since we fail. He would not be able to pay the penalty humanity deserves for their sin. And his bodily resurrection requires him to be human if it is to give us assurance that we, too, will be raised bodily.

NOTE: The question of Jesus' divinity and humanity will be looked at in more detail in the second part of the DVD.

▶ **WATCH DVD 2.2** (8 min 28 sec) **OR DELIVER TALK 2.2** (see page 50)

* *Encourage the group to make notes as they watch the DVD or listen to the talk. There is space for notes on page 32 of the Handbook.*

Discuss

1. **Jesus is God in the flesh.**
2. **Jesus is the resurrected King.**
3. **Jesus is the truth-telling Lord.**
4. **Jesus is the sin-bearing Savior.**
5. **Jesus is the only way.**

What is the good news for us in each of these statements?

1. We can know the truth about God because he has shown us what he is like in Christ.
2. Death is not the end. Jesus' death on the cross "worked." The world is not random, but ruled. A judgment is coming that will leave no wrong unpunished.
3. We can know the truth about God and ourselves from a reliable source.
4. Our sins can be forgiven. God's love for us is beyond all our wildest dreams.
5. There is a way back to God, through grace, not works. We can have assurance of our acceptance with God through Christ.

Which of these came across to you most powerfully when you first heard the gospel?

Your group may have a variety of answers to this question. As well as helping group members get to know each other better, this will begin to open up the fact that non-Christians will also be particularly struck by one or two of these five truths about Jesus. Bear in mind that some of your group may not be able to look back at a specific moment when they first heard the gospel. If they grew up in a Christian family, and can't remember a time when they didn't know and love Jesus, ask them if they were particularly struck by one aspect of Jesus' identity as they got older.

Are there any you only heard/appreciated later on? What impact did that have on you?

Some may have had the experience of only being told a "partial gospel." For example, an emphasis on Jesus being our Savior and Friend, but little if anything said about him being Lord and King. This will likely have a negative impact later on, because this person hasn't been challenged with the lordship of Christ over their lives. They haven't fully counted the cost of being a Christian. Equally, there can be a great focus on Christ's rule, but not on his mercy—meaning that someone may lack assurance of forgiveness and acceptance.

"The gospel message, at its most simple, is this—Jesus is Lord."
From what you have heard in this session, how might you unpack the phrase "Jesus is Lord" to explain what it means?

Whole books could be filled unpacking this phrase! The key is to focus both on "Jesus" (a human name for a real human, meaning "God saves"—pointing to the reason for the coming to earth of God the Son), and on "Lord" (a term reserved for addressing God, pointing to the divinity, power and rule of Jesus). Put simply, the gospel is that this man Jesus is both Rescuer and Ruler.

So answers from the group may include:
- Only Jesus is Lord—no one and nothing else. And he is the way God saves his people so that they can live under his rule.
- Jesus Christ, who was born as a baby in Bethlehem 2,000 years ago and lived as a human, is Lord and Savior of all.
- Jesus is Lord—he always has been, is now, and always will be, and he came to save his people.

You could use the verses below to help you.

ROMANS 10:9

If you confess with your mouth that Jesus is Lord and believe in your heart that God raised him from the dead, you will be saved.

COLOSSIANS 1:19

For in him all the fullness of God was pleased to dwell.

JOHN 1:3

All things were made through him, and without him was not any thing made that was made.

MATTHEW 1:21

You shall call his name Jesus, for he will save his people from their sins.

"If we don't talk about Jesus, we are adding noise to a confused conversation." Look at the following statements. How could you turn these into conversations about Jesus?

"All religions are the same, so it doesn't matter which you believe."

Jesus himself made it very clear that he is the only way to be in a right relationship with God (John 14:6). Jesus says that religions are not all the same. If Jesus is the truth about God, he is where we need to look for our information about God. We do not need to, and would be wrong to, look anywhere else.

"I try to treat people the way I'd want to be treated. I reckon I've lived an OK life."

What we look like on the outside can be very different to what we are like on the inside. No matter how hard we try to live an "OK life," we still have thoughts and desires that we wouldn't want anyone else to see. Jesus knows that this is what we are really like, and that these things "defile us" (make us unfit for God). We might read out or quote the following passage to someone:

20 And he said, "What comes out of a person is what defiles him. 21 For from within, out of the heart of man, come evil thoughts, sexual immorality, theft, murder, adultery, 22 coveting, wickedness, deceit, sensuality, envy, slander, pride, foolishness. 23 All these evil things come from within, and they defile a person." (Mark 7 v 20-23)

"My friend says that when we die, we come back as someone else. I hope I'll be rich next time."

How can we know for sure what happens when we die? Only by asking someone who's died! Jesus died and was raised to new life. In the most famous verse in the Bible, Jesus says that what happens after death depends on whether or not we believe in him: *"For God so loved the world, that he gave his only Son, that whoever believes in him should not perish but have eternal life"* (John 3:16).

Jesus said that true wealth is not in human belongings but in being rich toward God (Matthew 6:19-20).

The rest of the Bible is also clear about what happens when we die: *"For the wages of sin is death, but the free gift of God is eternal life in Christ Jesus our Lord"* (Romans 6:23).

Pray

Look again at the list on page 33 [of the Handbook]. **Thank Jesus for being each one of these things.**

Think of the person who first told you the gospel message or helped you understand it more fully. Thank God for bringing that person into your life so that you could know the truth about the Lord Jesus.

Pray that you will grow in your knowledge and love of Jesus, and that you will want to share that joy with other people.

DAILY BIBLE DEVOTIONALS

Remind group members about the daily devotionals they can do at home over the course of the next week. This week the devotionals focus on the aspects of Jesus' identity highlighted in the main teaching session, from the Gospel of Matthew.

SERMONS

OPTION ONE: JOHN 10:11-33

In this session Erik focuses on a variety of passages to unpack various key aspects of Jesus' identity. He uses John 10:17-18 to show us that Jesus is the truth-telling Lord—this passage includes those verses and also teaches several other aspects Erik points to, including the purpose of Christ's death (v 11), the reality of his resurrection (v 17-18), his unique ability to give eternal life (v 28), and his divinity (v 30-33).

OPTION TWO: COLOSSIANS 1:15-23

This is the passage the Bible study is based on (see next page), which could also be expanded upon in a sermon.

OPTION THREE: REVELATION 1:9-19

This vision of Jesus given to John on Patmos is not mentioned in this material, but picks up on several of the themes of this session, especially:
- The humanity and divinity of Jesus (v 12-17).
- The death-defeating death and resurrection of Jesus (v 18).
- The authority over the present and the future of Jesus (v 19).

If one of your Sunday sermons is to be based on the theme of this session, church members will find a page to write notes on the sermon on page 43 of their Handbooks.

AIM: The main teaching session for this week focused on explaining some core truths about Jesus Christ. The aim of this Bible study is to reinforce these truths from a single passage. Your group members should finish this study with a deep sense of awe at how amazing the Lord Jesus really is—and a sense of privilege that we get to tell the world about him.

Discuss

What popular films or TV portrayals of Jesus have you seen recently. How do you think these have helped or hindered our understanding of Jesus' true identity and mission?

What value (if any) do you think there is in such attempts to portray Christ?

You might show a clip of a film to start off this discussion. Films can help people appreciate that Jesus was both real and fully human, but in general, film portrayals of Christ tend to reinforce cultural stereotypes, and focus attention on the wrong things—clothing, facial expressions and hairstyles, rather than his teaching, character and power. Some or all of your group may object strongly to images of Jesus, so be sensitive about how you handle this. "Blessed are those who have not seen, and yet have believed!" (John 20 v 29).

OPTIONAL: Real or fake? Show the group a series of pictures and ask them to decide which is real and which is fake. Just google "real or fake photos" to get to some fun quiz sites. The aim is to get your group thinking about real and fake versions of things.

READ COLOSSIANS 1:15-23

¹⁵ He is the image of the invisible God, the firstborn of all creation...

1. **Notice the number of times that Paul uses the words "all," "everything" and "fullness". What big point is he making in this passage?**

Jesus is fully sufficient for everything! He is both fully God and fully man. He is Lord of all. He is Lord of the church and all creation. Our temptation is always to think that Jesus is smaller than the world, the dark forces of evil, ourselves or great and powerful human institutions. We are wrong. Jesus Christ is Lord over all these things, and therefore completely sufficient for everything we need for salvation, life and eternity.

2. Which verses show that Jesus is fully God, and which show that he is also fully man?

Fully God: Verse 15: "image," "firstborn" (=son and heir). Verse 16: "all things were created through him and for him." Verse 19: "in him all the fullness of God was pleased to dwell," and many more...
Fully man: Verse 20: "blood of his cross." Verse 22: "body of flesh," "death."
All these words, concepts and phrases show the physical reality of Jesus' human life and body. This is a vital doctrine to understand and hold to, as our salvation depends upon it. Jesus needed to be a man to die as our representative. And as God, Jesus bore the penalty of sin. It was not a random third party who paid the price, but God himself.

How would you explain to someone who isn't a Christian that Jesus is the "image" of God?

When we look at Jesus we see God. For most people, the truth about God and life after death is a matter of opinion. Now that Jesus has come, all the guessing games about God are at an end. What Jesus teaches, God teaches. What he does, God does. Who he is, God is. We might use picture language to explain it to people (after all, Paul uses a visual image!)—Jesus is a window into God. He reflects God's character and will perfectly. But it is also important to underline that Jesus is not just a reflection or a two-dimensional picture of a three-dimensional God. As the passage goes on to explain, he is the image of God because all the fullness of God lives in him (v 19).

3. Most people in the west think the universe came about by chance, and is sustained by the laws of physics. What would Paul say about that (see v 15-17)?

Jesus is both the means by which the world came into being, *and* the reason why it keeps going. Physical laws may describe how something works as it does, but the Bible reveals the who and the why of creation. It was made by Jesus and for him. Jesus is the answer to the meaning of our existence. You could discuss how this can be a helpful topic in evangelistic conversations. It might be worth noting that any discussions we have about the origins of life, evolution and creation need to lead to and focus on the person and work of Christ; otherwise we are not really telling the gospel.

4. What is the natural state of human beings (v 21, see also v 13)? How have you seen this in your own life, and in the lives of people you know?

We were God's enemies, alienated (separated) from him and antagonistic in the way we thought about God. By implication from verse 22, we were also unholy, blameworthy and without hope before his judgment. Verse 13 adds the spiritual dimension that we were also members of the dark kingdom of the devil.

This is powerful language to describe what is often shown in very ordinary ways by those who are not yet Christians. There are some Christian biographies that describe people who hit the depths of depravity. For many people, however, their enmity and hatred toward God is shown by indifference, a critical spirit, or self-righteousness. People may be warm, kind, generous and "moral," while at the same time enemies of the gospel.

5. How does Jesus' death on the cross deal with this (v 20, 22)?

People are hostile to God, but because of their sin, God is also their enemy. Jesus' death brings peace by ending the war from God's side, making it possible for people to be reconciled to him. That it took Jesus' death to achieve this shows how enormous the gulf is between man and God. In Christ we can approach God as holy, blameless and above reproach (v 22).

How would you explain to someone what it means that the cross brings peace?

If people do not know how to explain the cross using "the swap," "the book," or "the chairs" illustrations, demonstrate one or more to your group. These explanations can be downloaded from www.gospelshapedchurch.org/outreach.

6. **What happens when someone responds to the message about Jesus (v 20-23, see also v 13)?**

We are reconciled to God (v 20); we are at peace with God (v 20); we are made holy in his sight (v 22); we are rescued from the kingdom of darkness (v 13).

So why is it such a privilege to be a "minister" or servant of the gospel (v 23)?

We get to hold out the message that is the only thing that offers any hope for mankind (v 23). Being gospel sharers draws us into God's great plan for the universe. We are privileged to be part of a worldwide scheme that involves everyone. We are serving the only Person and project that will make a difference to people's lives for eternity.

7. **How should people respond to Christ (v 23)? Who is the "you" Paul is addressing in this verse?**

We respond by listening to, understanding and believing the message. But notice that how you enter is also how you progress and grow. This is not just a once-for-all experience; we are to refresh and renew our understanding and exercise faith in the gospel on an ongoing basis. We are made alive by the gospel, but we also live and grow by the gospel. See Colossians 2:6-7. This verse is addressed to Christians as much as to non-Christians.

Apply

FOR YOURSELF: The gospel message is all about Jesus—who he is and what he has done. What are some of the less offensive aspects of the Christian life that we are tempted to talk about instead of Jesus?

We would rather talk about "God" or our church, or about "values," or even about our own testimony or experience of God. None of these things are wrong in and of themselves, but they must lead on to talking about Jesus— who he is and what he has done.

How can we help ourselves and each other to talk more about Jesus?

Share some thoughts with each other about how we can be encouraged to talk about Jesus. Here are some ideas—you will have plenty more:

- Keep reminding yourself and each other that Jesus is the gospel.
- Mention Christ early on in a conversation. It gets more difficult the longer you leave it.
- Try to answer questions by recounting stories from Jesus' life. Quote Jesus' teaching as: "Jesus said..." rather than: "The Bible says..."
- Make conversations about God, church, or your own experience point toward Jesus, rather than staying silent about him.
- "I discovered the truth about God when I realized that Jesus was the place to look for the answers about him..."
- "I go to a church that is convinced that Jesus is where we need to look for answers about truth, God and the meaning of our lives..."

FOR YOUR CHURCH: Look back over the five aspects of who Jesus is and what he has done on page 33 [of the Handbook]. Do you think your church emphasizes one of the aspects over the others? Are there any aspects of his identity that you might be in danger of neglecting? Why is that—and what is the remedy?

For good reasons, churches can focus more heavily on one aspect of Jesus' person and work—often because there is a specific error in the church or the culture that needs to be refuted. But this can sometimes lead to the neglect of other aspects of the truth, or even suspicion about those which have become the focus for error. For example, Jesus' substitutionary death has been a particular focus of many evangelical churches recently, because it has been under attack by liberals and others. It has been right to preach and teach about it. But when it is the focus of teaching to the exclusion of other truths, a church is in danger of becoming unbalanced itself.

The remedy is partly to recognize this effect, and to continue to teach "the whole counsel of God" (Acts 20:27). Systematic exposition of the Bible in sermon series and in group Bible studies helps prevent a church from becoming obsessed with one doctrine at the expense of others.

Pray

- *Don't forget to ask if there have been any answers to your prayers for gospel opportunities this week.*

    Spend some time worshiping the Lord together in words—using the passage as a basis for your thanks and praise.

- *Keep your Bibles open for this, and quote words and phrases from the passage to start your prayers. This is a thoroughly biblical way of praying together—using God's word to shape and form our prayers and praises.*

    FOR THE GROUP: Ask God to give you each a bigger vision for who Jesus is and what he has done for you.

    FOR YOUR WHOLE CHURCH: Pray that working through this curriculum would be a constructive exercise for your church. Pray for unity and for your leaders. And pray that the end result will be that your church is more committed to gospel-shaped outreach.

FURTHER READING

To evangelize is to spread the good news that Jesus Christ died for our sins and was raised from the dead according to the Scriptures, and that as the reigning Lord he now offers the forgiveness of sins and the liberating gift of the Spirit to all who repent and believe.

John Stott

We are not called to proclaim philosophy and metaphysics, but the simple gospel. Man's fall, his needs of a new birth, forgiveness through atonement, and salvation as a result of faith, these are our battle-axe and weapons of war.

C.H. Spurgeon

I have but one passion: It is he, it is he alone. The world is the field and the field is the world; and henceforth that country shall be my home where I can be most used in winning souls for Christ.

Nikolaus Ludwin von Zinzendorf

Books

- *Jesus the King (Tim Keller)*
- *The Cross of Christ (John Stott)*
- *Scandalous: The Cross and Resurrection of Jesus (Don Carson)*
- *What is the Gospel? (Greg Gilbert)*
- *Original Jesus (Carl Laferton)*
- *Stop Asking Jesus into your Heart (J.D. Greear)*

Online

- *Jesus did More to Save Us than Die:* gospelshapedchurch.org/resources221
- *Jesus is Fully Human: gospelshapedchurch.org/resources222*

LEADER'S REFLECTIONS

SESSION 3:
WHO ARE WE?

WE'VE CONSIDERED WHO JESUS IS — GOD IN THE
FLESH, THE RESURRECTED KING, THE TRUTH-TELLING
LORD, THE SIN-BEARING SAVIOR AND THE ONLY WAY
TO BE RIGHT WITH GOD. THE HEART OF THE GOSPEL
MESSAGE IS JESUS. NOW WE MOVE ON TO LOOK AT
THE HEARTS OF THE MESSENGERS — US, AND OUR
CHURCH. IT IS NOT ONLY JESUS' IDENTITY THAT WE
NEED TO APPRECIATE — IT IS OURS, TOO.

TALK OUTLINE

3.1 ● Believers in the church should see themselves as a missionary family, whose family business is making and training disciples.

● **THE BASIS OF A MISSIONARY FAMILY** *Matthew 28:18-20; John 20:21*
God is building a new family, the church. We have the same...
 • **History:** sin and separation from God.
 • **Experience of salvation:** repentance and faith in Christ.
 • **Future:** God's eternal kingdom.
 • **Commission:** to make and train disciples.

3.2 ● **THE ENEMY OF A MISSIONARY FAMILY** *John 14:15*
 • The heart of the gospel is selfless love; the enemy of living like Jesus is selfishness.
 • The root of all sin is loving ourselves.
 • If we're not living as a missionary family, the issue is our own selfishness. We are not loving God and we are not loving others.

● **THE SUSTAINMENT OF A MISSIONARY FAMILY**
 • Loving service is at the heart of evangelism.
 • We need to be shaped by God's word day by day.
 • We're here to give ourselves. We serve others by sharing the gospel.

● **THE PRACTICE OF A MISSIONARY FAMILY** *Matthew 28:18-20; John 20:21*
 • What would change about your life if you did your current job as a missionary overseas?
 • Jesus has sent us into the world as his missionaries. This is our identity.

● **CONCLUSION:** We are missionaries sent by a missionary God. Do you know who you really are? Does anything need to change in your life to reflect this identity?

You can download a full transcript of these talks at
WWW.GOSPELSHAPEDCHURCH.ORG/OUTREACH/TALKS

WHO ARE WE?

* *Ask the group members to turn to Session 3 on page 45 of the Handbook.*

Discuss

Talk about any missionaries you know. What do you imagine their lives are like from day to day?

Don't spend too long on this question; it's simply an easy introduction to the concept of what a missionary is and does.

Can you come up with a simple definition of what a missionary is?

This is not a trick question! If your group comes up with a definition that assumes missionaries will work overseas, that's fine. They will still be able to apply the definition to their own lives later on when we discuss the fact that all Christians are to be missionaries.

▶ **WATCH DVD 3.1** (3 min 52 sec) **OR DELIVER TALK 3.1** (see page 68)

* *Encourage the group to make notes as they watch the DVD or listen to the talk. There is space for notes on page 47 of the Handbook.*

Discuss

What did Roger say was the most discouraging thing on the mission field? If you were supporting a missionary who was like this, what would you say to them?

Roger said the most discouraging aspect of ministry in his region is the other missionaries. He says:

"Many western churches send people to their area for mission work but in reality they are just on a vacation. They collect a check, get the benefits, and relax at the beach. Their engagement with the locals is minimal and when they do engage

69

with them, a critical spirit often accompanies it. These 'missionaries' take up space at church and are really not willing to serve."

● *Ask your group what they would say (or want to say) to a missionary they were supporting, if the missionary was behaving like this.*

Encourage group members to be honest about what they would want to say, even if church structures mean it would actually be someone else who was given the task of addressing this with the missionary. It would be great if the group were to express a sense of anger at the way their support was being misused.

"Believers in the church should see themselves as a missionary family—and the family business is making and training disciples." How did you react to this statement?

Help group members to see that there are two aspects to being part of a missionary family:

1. Individual believers are missionaries. As we saw in Session 1, all of us have the responsibility and privilege of telling others the good news about Jesus Christ. So, we are a family made up of missionaries.

2. The church—God's people together—also has a mission focus. The church is God's way of showcasing the gospel to the rest of the world. As people see Christians of all shapes and sizes meeting together and loving each other, they see the gospel at work (John 13:34-35). So, we are a missionary family.

What are some of the reasons why individual believers and whole churches can lose their focus on reaching out to others?

In Session 1 we noted that new believers rarely need to be reminded to tell other people about Jesus—because the good news feels very good to them. But over time, evangelism can become less of a reflex and more of a challenge. In addition, other things can begin to crowd in and fill our lives with busyness. This can be true for churches as well, with programs, events and the day-to-day business of church pushing out our focus on evangelism.

WATCH DVD 3.2 (4 min 26 sec) OR DELIVER TALK 3.2 (see page 68)

* *Encourage the group to make notes as they watch the DVD or listen to the talk. There is space for notes on page 49 of the Handbook.*

Discuss

"The enemy of evangelism is selfishness." In what ways have you seen this to be true in your own life?

Be ready to give an example of your own to start the discussion if no one else volunteers an answer. Don't spend too long on this question, so that you have time for the following one, which will focus on positive things we can do rather than negative things we may have been doing up until now.

"Loving service is the heart of evangelism". How would things look different in our own lives and in our church if we were motivated by loving service, rather than selfishness?

We love God by being obedient to his command to love one another and to spread the gospel message. We love others by wanting what is best for them and working for it. What is truly best for others is that they know Christ and find forgiveness and eternal life through him. Use this discussion as a way to focus on some things that you can change quite quickly, and on others that you can start now but which may take longer.

MATTHEW 28:19

"Go therefore and make disciples of all nations."

"All nations" includes *your* nation, so discuss the same questions that Erik asked his friend: *"What would change about your life if you did your current job as a missionary in another country? What changes would you make if you had been sent to a foreign country, and given a job, a house and the mandate to be a missionary and reach those people?"*

There are a lot of questions here, so you may want to choose two or three to focus on. Alternatively, ask the group to spend a few minutes quietly working through the list themselves, writing in their answers as they apply each question to their own lives.

- **How would you spend your time?**
- **How would you pray?**
- **What types of relationships would you pursue?**
- **How would you read the news?**
- **What would you think of your neighbors?**
- **How would you talk to the cashiers at the local supermarket?**
- **What would you be listening for in your community?**

You may want to explain the last question. "What would you be listening for in your community?" refers to getting a feel for the people and area you are in, eg: what local issues are people interested in? What is the make-up of the community in terms of ethnic background, education, religion, culture, etc?

What practical things can we do to keep showing each other and encouraging each other that we are part of a missionary family?

You might get a long list of possible ideas, which would be good to write down to think about later. But it is important that you focus on at least one thing people can do as individuals, and one you could do together as a church. If the suggestion for something to do as a church will need to be agreed by the church leadership, tell the group that you will pass the idea on to the relevant leader.

Pray

Pray for the missionaries you thought about at the beginning of this session. Now pray for yourselves as missionaries, and your church as a missionary family. Look again at the answers you gave to the final question above. Ask God to help you put these things into action.

DAILY BIBLE DEVOTIONALS

This week's daily Bible devotionals walk through 1 Peter 1 – 2, showing us the church's identity and how declaring God's excellence to the world is at the heart of God's purpose for his church.

SERMONS

OPTION ONE: JOHN 20:19-23

This is one of the passages Erik looks at in his DVD presentation, which could be expanded upon in a sermon.

OPTION TWO: ACTS 4:18-31

This is one of the passages the Bible study is based on (see next page), which could also be expanded upon in a sermon.

OPTION THREE: 2 KINGS 7:3-16

This passage is not mentioned in this material, but picks up on the key points that as God's people, we are those who are together given:
- the blessing of enjoying the victory God has won for us (v 5-8).
- the duty to go and tell the good news of that victory (v 9-11).

If one of your Sunday sermons is to be based on the theme of this session, church members will find a page to write notes on the sermon on page 59 of their Handbooks.

AIM: The main teaching session for this week focused on establishing our identity as missionaries. The aim of this Bible study is to reinforce this truth from two passages in Acts. Your group members should finish this study with a much stronger sense that they are part of a family on a mission, and that our lives both as individuals and as a group should be focused on that mission.

Discuss

"The church is..." How might people finish that sentence if you asked a random selection of strangers in the street?

You would get a range of answers, both friendly and hostile. There would be some who think that the church is an outdated, irrelevant institution; some who focus on the building; others who focus on the positive social things the church is involved in, or the kindness of members; and others who would talk about hypocrisy and what they perceive as bigoted attitudes. The vast majority would view it as a human institution ruled by people.

How would *you* finish that sentence?

Apart from emotional value-judgements (great, exciting, a bit boring), we are looking for group members to identify some key features:
- formed and owned by God (not a human institution)
- a fellowship of believers (not a building)
- a group with a mission in the world: to worship and honor God by modeling grace and reaching out with the gospel of Christ.

If you don't get good answers to this second part, don't worry—just move on. The key features of this question will be picked up in the Bible study.

☞ READ ACTS 2:42-47

42 And they devoted themselves to the apostles' teaching and the fellowship, to the breaking of bread and the prayers...

1. **Pick out some key characteristics of the church that Jesus formed by his Holy Spirit in the first few months after Pentecost.**

   - They were a devoted community (v 42)—they were committed to each other and learning from the apostles' teaching.
   - They were a loving community (v 44-45).
   - They were a worshiping community (v 46-47).
   - They were an evangelistic community (v 47).

2. **What would it have been like to be part of that first church? What would particularly attract you to join it?**

   Most people will think it would have been extremely exciting—not just for the miraculous signs but for the "buzz" of excitement about being part of a growing, committed family.

   Do you feel the same way about your own church? Why or why not?

   There may be a range of answers to this question. Some people will be very excited; others will be less enthusiastic. The key thing to underline with your group is that "fixing" this problem is not about getting the minister to preach better sermons, or changing the music, or the structures. It's about our individual and corporate devotion to the life and mission of the church, which will enable us to be the church we could be under God.

3. **What was the cause of the spectacular growth of this church family?**

   God's blessing through the Holy Spirit as the gospel was preached. But notice that a learning, worshiping, devoted, loving group of disciples is extremely attractive. The miraculous signs may have given authority to the message; but the message was endorsed and embodied by the changed lives of the believers.

4. **How did their life together support and complement the preaching of the good news about Jesus?**

   Their devotion to God and to one another made them an attractive community. They modeled in their love and generosity God's love and generosity, which is at the heart of the gospel. They were a living illustration of the gospel message they were proclaiming.

But the admiration of the church didn't last for long. Acts 3 – 4 recounts how, after Peter and John had spectacularly healed a disabled man in the name of Jesus, they were arrested, flogged, and warned not to speak about Christ any more. This was their response...

READ ACTS 4:18-31

5. When they are threatened, what do they do in response? Do you think this was easy for them?

- They refused to stop, saying that they were simply unable to lie about what they had seen and heard (v 20).
- They shared it with the fellowship (v 23).
- They prayed together for God's strength to continue (v 24, 29-30).

We sometimes think that the first disciples "had it easy." Peter and John needed the support of their fellowship, and the strength that only the Holy Spirit can give, in order to continue their outreach in the face of opposition.

6. What can we learn from their prayer that would encourage us to be a fellowship devoted to outreach—even against strong opposition?

- God is in control of everything (v 24)—we can trust him even when things seem to go horribly "wrong."
- Jesus' death is an example of God's sovereign will to complete his work of salvation against opposition (v 27). Even when the massive forces of military might and political power are against us, they will ultimately fail if we are being obedient to the call of the Lord.
- They appeal for God to be at work, but at the same time they do not neglect to do the work of outreach. They still need "to continue to speak [God's] word with all boldness" (v 29).

7. How is their prayer answered (v 31)?

The house shakes and they are filled with the Holy Spirit. Notice what being filled with the Spirit produces—they "continued to speak the word of God with boldness." Not a one-off event, but a continuing culture of whole-church outreach. John Chrysostom, the 4th-century Archbishop of Constantinople, observed: *"They were shaken so that they would be unshaken"* (Homily 11).

Apply

FOR MYSELF: Am I devoted to my church—its teaching, fellowship, mission, mutual care and generosity? Are there areas of church life where I am basically selfish, looking for what I can get out of it rather than what I can give to it?

Underline with your group members that we principally reform the church by *being* devoted church members.

FOR YOUR CHURCH: How can we as a fellowship grow to be more like the picture of a "missionary family" that we see in these passages? Think of some practical steps you might take together.

Get the group to focus on qualities, rather than specifics, and avoid complex discussions about signs and wonders, or the common ownership of goods. We can:
- encourage one another toward generosity, mutual love and practical care.
- make sure that we are focused on the important things, not distracted by petty squabbles, but on gratitude to God for our new life in Christ.
- allow the grace of God in Christ to shape our life together by devoting ourselves to hearing God's word together, and reminding each other about the good news of the gospel.
- make evangelism a priority for prayer.
- keep reminding each other that we are a missional community. It is our main job as individuals and as a church together to reach out with the gospel.
- make sure that as a church we are providing opportunities for evangelism together.

Pray

Spend some time thanking God for the way he has drawn you into the fellowship of your church with one another, and for what he is doing through you in the world.

FOR THE GROUP: Share the names of two people you know who you would like an opportunity to share the gospel with—a family member, a friend at work or a neighbor. Pray very specifically for boldness to talk with them about Christ.

FOR YOUR WHOLE CHURCH: Pray that you would encourage each other to be a "missionary family" week by week. And that you would grow together as a generous, loving, attractive family.

FURTHER READING

> *Every man is a missionary, now and forever, for good or for evil, whether he intends or designs it or not. He may be a blot ... or he may be a blessing ... but a blank he cannot be.*
> **Thomas Chalmers**

> *The Church exists for nothing else but to draw men into Christ ... if they are not doing that, all the cathedrals, clergy, missions, sermons, even the Bible itself, are simply a waste of time. God became Man for no other purpose.*
> **C.S. Lewis**

> *Some wish to live within the sound of a chapel bell; I wish to run a rescue mission within a yard of hell.*
> **C.T. Studd**

Books

- *The Mission of God's People: A Biblical Theology of the Church's Mission* (Christopher Wright)
- *Evangelism: How the Whole Church Speaks of Jesus* (Mack Stiles)
- *The Best-Kept Secret of Christian Mission* (John Dickson)

Autobiographies and biographies of missionaries:
- *Shadow of the Almighty: The Life and Testament of Jim Elliot* (Elisabeth Elliot)
- *Hudson Taylor* (J. Hudson Taylor)
- *God's Smuggler* (Brother Andrew and John Sherrill)
- *C.T. Studd: Cricketer and Pioneer* (Norman Grubb)
- *Adoniram Judson: Devoted for Life* (Vance Christie)

Online

- *Evangelism and the Sunday Morning Pulpit:* gospelshapedchurch.org/resources231

LEADER'S REFLECTIONS

SESSION 4:

WHO ARE WE REACHING?

IF WE ARE TO BE EFFECTIVE WITNESSES FOR CHRIST,
THEN WE NEED TO KNOW NOT ONLY ABOUT HIM, AND
ABOUT OURSELVES, BUT ABOUT THE PEOPLE WE LONG
TO TALK TO ABOUT HIM. IN THIS SESSION, WE SHALL
DISCOVER HOW JESUS SAW THOSE AROUND HIM, AND
CONSIDER HOW THAT SHOULD SHAPE OUR ATTITUDES
AND ACTIONS AS HIS PEOPLE.

TALK OUTLINE

4.1 • We should be motivated to evangelize by compassion—living as an unbeliever is very difficult. *(Share an example of a person who seemed to have it all, but whose life was empty of meaning.)*
Our default reaction is often condescension or apathy, but these lack love.

• **THE FACT OF THE CONDITION** *Ephesians 2:1-3*
Prior to our conversion, we were dead in our sin, absolutely alienated from God. Is this how we see unbelievers, including those we know personally?

• **THE EXPRESSION OF THE CONDITION** *Romans 1:18-23*
Sinful actions flow from suppressing the truth about God and worshiping created things. When we think of unbelievers, we must primarily think of what they *are* (separated from God), not what they *do*.

4.2 • **THE SYMPATHY FOR THE CONDITION** *Matthew 9:35-38*
• Jesus sees the crowds are harassed and helpless, and reacts with **compassion**. We must show the same love.
• Unbelievers are **hungry**: they cannot find satisfaction in created things.
• Unbelievers are **hurting**: the guilt of not being right with God is painful.
• Jesus' prayer is for laborers who reflect his compassionate, loving heart.

• **THE BURDEN FOR THE CONDITION** *1 Corinthians 6:9-11*
There is no place for feeling superior to unbelievers; we needed, and still need, the gospel just as much.

• **CONCLUSION:** Scripture teaches that the world around us is hungry and hurting. The compassionate response is to open our mouths and explain the gospel.

You can download a full transcript of these talks at
WWW.GOSPELSHAPEDCHURCH.ORG/OUTREACH/TALKS

WHO ARE WE REACHING?

* Ask the group members to turn to Session 4 on page 61 of the Handbook.

Discuss

What are some of the different labels we give to people who are not Christians?

> Answers could include: non-Christians, unbelievers, pagans, atheists, agnostics, the lost, skeptics, seekers.

How do these affect how we view them and relate to them?

> Ask the group whether different "labels" change how we think about people. For example:
> * do we expect a "skeptic" to be aggressive and to attack Christian beliefs?
> * do we find ourselves looking down on "pagans" and assuming their lifestyles are particularly ungodly?
> * do we feel an "atheist" is unlikely to be open to the gospel?

▶ **WATCH DVD 4.1** (8 min 21 sec) **OR DELIVER TALK 4.1** (see page 84)

* Encourage the group to make notes as they watch the DVD or listen to the talk. There is space for notes on page 63 of the Handbook.

Discuss

Without Christ, people are dead in their sins, walking in the way of the world and enslaved to the evil one (see Ephesians 2:1-3).

Why do we find it difficult to see people in the way the Bible describes them?

We tend to see people in terms of what they *do* rather than what they *are*. So, if people do kind, loving, generous things, it's easy to see them as nice, good people, rather than as being separated from God.

We also "compensate" for people we know well and love. We can start to gloss over the realities with our children, family members or other friends with whom we have a long-term relationship.

How can we help ourselves to see unbelievers through God's eyes?

Read some of the relevant Bible passages slowly and thoughtfully, while keeping in mind some of the non-Christians you know. Ask God to show you the truth of his words as you read. For example, read Ephesians 2:1-3 and Romans 3:10-12.

Christians can be condescending toward unbelievers, or apathetic about their condition. Which of these attitudes do you think you are more likely to fall into, and why?

Encourage group members to be honest in their answers. On the DVD, Erik explains condescension like this: "*Sometimes we look down at unbelievers as those who are not as spiritually smart as we are. We say: 'How can they live like that?' We shake our heads in despair at their lives—but then do nothing about it.*" We may fall into this attitude if we think people have already had plenty of opportunities to hear the gospel.

We may fall into apathy if we don't truly believe that unbelievers are not only separated from God now, but also face his righteous judgment when they die.

What happens when a church as a whole exhibits one or other of these traits, or both?

If a church is condescending toward unbelievers, they won't work as hard at making the gospel message crystal clear and engaging. Sermons will talk about non-Christians in judgmental or disparaging ways. If they are apathetic, they will not spend time and resources reaching out to unbelievers, but will, instead, expect non-Christians to make the effort themselves to come to church and find out more. The church will be inward-looking.

What is the solution to these ungodly attitudes?

- Repent and ask God's forgiveness.
- Ask God to help us as individuals and as a church to see unbelievers through his eyes, and to have compassion for them.
- Ask God to renew our passion for reaching any we may have given up on in the past.
- Review our church's evangelistic program to ensure it is clear and engaging, and reaches as widely as possible.

▶ **WATCH DVD 4.2** (7 min 13 sec) **OR DELIVER TALK 4.2** (see page 84)

- *Encourage the group to make notes as they watch the DVD or listen to the talk. There is space for notes on page 65 of the Handbook.*

Discuss

👉 MATTHEW 9:35-38

[35] And Jesus went throughout all the cities and villages, teaching in their synagogues and proclaiming the gospel of the kingdom and healing every disease and every affliction. [36] When he saw the crowds, he had compassion for them, because they were harassed and helpless, like sheep without a shepherd. [37] Then he said to his disciples, "The harvest is plentiful, but the laborers are few; [38] therefore pray earnestly to the Lord of the harvest to send out laborers into his harvest."

What drives Jesus' compassion for people?

He sees that the crowds are "harassed and helpless, like sheep without a shepherd."

"Harassed," "helpless," "sheep without a shepherd." Can you see how this is a good description for your friends and neighbors who are not Christians?

- They are **harassed** by false teaching from a world that makes empty promises.
- They are **helpless** because they look for answers to things and people that are broken.

- They are like **sheep without a shepherd** because they have no one to take care of them, or to point them to the hope and direction they need.

In the passage above, what does Jesus' love for the people cause him to do?

It leads him to tell the disciples to pray earnestly for compassionate laborers who will labor to bring in the harvest—ie: speak the gospel and lead people to repentance and faith.

Are you tempted to think that some people are "beyond" the gospel message for any reason? Why is that thinking so wrong?

We may fall into the temptation of thinking some people are "too sinful" to be forgiven, "too proud" to ask for forgiveness, "too sure" of their own views to be willing to change, or "too good" to really need saving.

But, as we read in Romans 3 (you might like to ask your group to turn to the passage): *"There is no distinction: for all have sinned and fall short of the glory of God"* (v 22-23). This means other people are no more "beyond" the gospel than we were—we are all sinners. And we can all be justified by the same grace (v 24). We all stand in equal need of grace; that grace is offered to all of us; and God can work in the hardest, proudest or most sinful of people, as well as in the "nicest." We need to remember our own sinfulness, so that we think: "If God brought me to saving faith, he can do it in anyone!" We need to remember that the only sin that is not covered by the blood of Christ is if someone continues to reject Jesus as Lord and Savior, since he is the only means by which we may be saved.

When you first visited church, what was familiar to you? What was strange? What are you doing now to make visitors welcome, and your meetings understandable—whether or not they believe in Jesus?

We easily forget how strange church can be for those who have never been— the unfamiliar and technical language; handling multiple strange books; standing and sitting; singing together, etc. Even if the Sunday worship is primarily for believers, it should be accessible to those who are exploring or approaching Christian faith. We should never assume that people know which books to use, or when to stand and sit. We should also be more careful to explain the meaning of unfamiliar words.

Pray

Ask God to forgive you for times when you have failed to show true compassion to unbelievers; for example, through apathy, condescension or thinking they are beyond saving.

In Session 1 you were asked to think of two people you would like to share the gospel with this month (see page 18). Ask God to help you truly see these people in the way he sees them—as "harassed and helpless, like sheep without a shepherd."

Pray that you will see others more and more through biblical eyes, and that this will motivate you to tell them about Jesus.

DAILY BIBLE DEVOTIONALS

Do encourage your group members at the end of the main teaching session to keep studying, or start to study, the daily devotionals. This week they highlight the compassion of the Lord Jesus, seen in how he interacted with a variety of hungry, hurting people.

SERMONS

👉 OPTION ONE: MATTHEW 9:35-38

This is one of the passages Erik looks at in his DVD presentation, which could be expanded upon in a sermon.

👉 OPTION TWO: EPHESIANS 2:1-10

This is the passage the Bible study is based on (see next page), which could also be expanded upon in a sermon.

👉 OPTION THREE: GENESIS 3:1-24

This passage is not mentioned in this material, but has much to say about sin and judgment, and therefore about the lives of those around us. You could emphasize:

- The expression of sin—broken relationships and blame-shifting (v 7-13).
- The consequences of sin—God's judgment: life in a painful world, followed by death (v 16-19).
- The promise to sinners—provision for life, and defeat of the serpent and death (v 21, 15).

If one of your Sunday sermons is to be based on the theme of this session, church members will find a page to write notes on the sermon on page 75 of their Handbooks.

BIBLE STUDY

AIM: The main teaching session for this week focused on how we should view unbelievers, and the devotionals gave examples of how compassionate the Lord Jesus was in his encounters with people. This Bible study seeks to nail down how God sees unbelievers, and how we can more constructively communicate with them the liberating gospel of grace.

Discuss

Think about a major change that you have undergone in your life—from single to married; from study to work; from living with parents to living independently, etc. What were some of the big things you loved about your "new life"? What were some of the things you were previously concerned about that disappeared?

> This should be a fun conversation about change, and how things that seemed enormously important beforehand completely disappear once your new life starts. Try not to let the conversation go on too long!

 READ EPHESIANS 2:1-10

> [1] *And you were dead in the trespasses and sins...*

1. What three things do people who are not Christians follow, according to Paul?

   - The way of the world (v 2).
   - Satan (the prince of the power of the air) (v 2).
   - Their own passions and desires (v 3).

   This is the classic Christian formulation of "the world, the flesh and the devil."

2. What phrases describe the consequences of this way of thinking and living for the present (v 1), and the future (v 3)? What do these phrases actually mean?

- They are spiritually dead (v 1) now. This does not mean that they are physically dead, but spiritually dead and unresponsive toward God. Compare Adam and Eve in Genesis 3. The promise was that "in the day you eat of [the fruit] you shall surely die" (Genesis 2:17). They did not die physically that day, but became part of the world where sin and death reign.
- They are destined for judgment ("children of wrath," v 2) in the future. In other words, they will bear the punishment for their sins themselves in hell for all eternity.

Why is there no excuse for "walking" in sin?

People try to escape from the responsibility of their sin and transgression by saying: "The devil made me do it" or "I was just following along with everyone else." But verse 3 makes it clear that the devil tempts, and the world encourages us, to do the very things that we ourselves want to do—and we choose to do them. We are without excuse.

3. What does this way of living look like in the reality of people's daily lives?

It covers a huge range of possibilities—some people are outwardly moral, kind and upright. Others exhibit more obvious external signs of their sins and transgressions. But whatever people look like from the outside, they are, in reality, spiritually dead sinners, who are enslaved to their own passions.

It might be worth underlining the ordinariness of this kind of life. We simply do what we want to do; we partake of what is tempting to us; we do what everyone else does—often without much thought to the morality, the consequences or the value of it. The language Paul uses seems to be very strong—but it is not. It is just that we are so used to living this way, or regarding this way of living as "normal," that God's view of our lives seems shockingly stark by contrast.

Think back to before you were a Christian. In what ways can you now see that verses 1-3 were true of you?

Allow people to talk about their own experience, making sure that you connect them back to the passage.

How would you have responded back then to being described in this way?

This will help people to see that the gospel is offensive. Encourage them to think of how we can effectively communicate this truth in a helpful way.

4. **What three words does Paul use in verses 4-5 to describe the character of God? Explain what they mean from the passage.**

It is astonishing that God would have anything to do with such hopeless, ungrateful, sinful, disobedient creatures. But he does.

- **Love:** God has the reason and the right to judge us, but because of his great love for us, he chooses not to, but goes to enormous lengths and cost to rescue us instead.
- **Mercy:** God forgives us when we don't deserve it. He makes us alive when we are dead. He makes us children of God, not children of wrath.
- **Grace/kindness:** Undeserved favor. If mercy is not punishing us for what we do deserve, then grace is giving us what we do not deserve—life, riches, all the blessings that we have in Christ.

It might be appropriate to stop at this point in the study and spend time praising God for who he is, and what he has done for us in Christ.

5. **What three big things does God do for those he saves (v 5, 6, 10)? How should we feel about these?**

- He makes us alive in Christ (v 5).
- He raised us up to sit in heaven with Christ (v 6); ie: our life and our salvation is secure.
- He makes us new people in Christ, and gives us "good works" to do (v 10).

We should not feel proud—because it is all through grace by faith, not by our works. We should be filled with a deep sense of gratitude and thankfulness to God for what he has done for us; joyful at our privileged status; and filled with a desire to share this good news with others.

6. **How are people saved, and how are they not saved (v 8-9)?**

- By grace, through trusting the promise of God.
- Not by our own efforts, character, personality, gifts or otherwise.

How is it possible to be very religious and very spiritually dead?

Religion based on works is the default setting of the human heart. We think that God will like us if we serve him and do good things for him. But the gospel of grace teaches us that the opposite is true.

Even as believers, we too easily start to think that we were saved because of our own works or "loveability," rather than the love of God and the work of Christ in dying for us. The cure for this is to constantly "remember" who we were, and what the gospel is (see verses 11-13).

7. **How might remembering both how we were without Christ and what Christ has done for us help us as we speak to others about the gospel?**

    • We need to remember that the gospel is a foreign language to people. They are dead, but may not recognize it. They are under judgment, but may not be conscious of it. As we once were, they may not be aware of how much they need Christ. This understanding will help us as we try to find ways of conversing about Jesus that help them see these truths, as the Holy Spirit awakens a desire to know Christ in them.
    • When we remember that we were saved by love, it will help us to love those who are lost without Jesus.
    • When we remember that the gospel is by grace, we will stop making moralistic judgments about others, and seek to share the gospel with anyone and everyone.

Apply

FOR YOURSELF: It is easy to see people in general as an inconvenience, a way of getting what you want, or a way of making you happy or contented. What would change if you always saw unbelievers as hopeless and helpless sinners, who need to experience the love of God in Christ?

Encourage the group to be very practical in their answers.

FOR YOUR CHURCH: How would it help your church if they remembered and applied the following truths?

1. We were dead in sins (v 1).

Answers might include: explain the gospel clearly and carefully in our meetings for those who are present; sympathize with their inability to grasp the truths of the gospel; pray more for God to open their eyes and give them life.

2. People are by nature children of wrath (v 3).

Answers might include: a greater sense of urgency about gospeling activities—we are trying to rescue people from hell.

3. We have been saved by grace (v 8).

Our gospel-sharing should be joyful and grateful—not judgmental or mean-spirited. We should not impose any additional conditions on people in responding to the gospel, other than faith.

4. No one may boast (v 9).

Making sure that we do not sound superior in our preaching, announcements and other communications.

Pray

Talk about the people you prayed together for last week. Have there been any opportunities with them this week? Continue to pray for them.

FOR YOURSELF: Ask God to help you see others as he sees them. Ask that God would fill you with love and compassion for them.

FOR YOUR WHOLE CHURCH: Ask the Lord to help your church be loving toward those who are not yet Christians. Pray that outsiders will see the love, mercy and grace of God modeled in your life together.

FURTHER READING

How do we react to those around us? Do we see their success, their possessions, their confidence, all the things that are impressive? Or do we see that, deep down, they are harassed and helpless, wandering in what John Calvin called a 'ruinous labyrinth,' that exits only into death.
Rico Tice

God save us from living in comfort while sinners are sinking into hell!
C.H. Spurgeon

Books

- *Romans 1 – 7 For You*, chapters 2 – 5 (Tim Keller)
- *The Supremacy of Christ in a Postmodern World* (ed. John Piper & Justin Taylor)
- *Counterfeit Gods* (Tim Keller)
- *The Intolerance of Tolerance* (Don Carson)
- *Good News to the Poor* (Tim Chester)

Online

- *How Churches can Evangelize their Neighborhoods*: gospelshapedchurch.org. resources241
- *Four Lessons for Evangelism Across Economic Boundaries*: gospelshapedchurch.org/resources242
- *How to Share the Gospel with Muslims*: gospelshapedchurch.org/resources243

LEADER'S REFLECTIONS

SESSION 5:

WHAT IS THE GOSPEL PLAN?

THE GOSPEL IS ALL ABOUT THE LIFE, DEATH,
RESURRECTION AND RULE OF JESUS, GOD THE SON.
AND THIS GOSPEL IS GOD THE FATHER'S INITIATIVE –
HE SENT HIS SON TO BE HIS PEOPLE'S LORD AND
SAVIOR. SO WHEN DID THIS PLAN BEGIN? WHERE IS
IT ALL HEADING? AND HOW DOES THAT CHANGE HOW
WE VIEW OUR ROLE AS GOSPEL WITNESSES?

TALK OUTLINE

5.1 ● Every organization has a goal: God's big-picture plan for the church in our period of history is for us to make disciples.

● **GOSPEL BEGINNINGS** *Genesis 3, 11 and 12*
Adam and Eve rebelled against God. The consequences were:
• Vertical: separation from God.
• Horizontal: disharmony in relationships.
• Cosmic: felt by all of creation.
God promised that a descendant of Eve would conquer sin, Satan and death (3:15). God judged the disobedience of the people of Babel by scattering and confusing them (11:1-9). But God promised to bring blessing, favor and restoration to people from all nations, through a descendant of Abram (12:1-4).

5.2 ● **GOSPEL ENDINGS** *Revelation 5*
• As he sees a Jesus-given vision of heaven, John is distraught at the prospect of God's redemptive plan being frustrated. Would that make us cry?
• Only Jesus can open the scroll; only he can bring about God's salvation plan.
• Jesus is the offspring promised in Genesis 3:15.
• The response is to worship Jesus, for his worth and his work.
• God's gospel plan to bring salvation to all nations **will** be fulfilled; but how?

5.3 ● **GOSPEL WORKERS** Matthew 28:19-20
• Jesus' command to make disciples is the center of what a church should be.
• The gospel message is for **everyone**—it reverses Babel by breaking down ethnic barriers.
• We can have confidence because Jesus has authority. Our job is to talk to people about Jesus, not convert them—that's above our pay grade.
• Jesus promises to stand with us in our evangelistic task.

● **CONCLUSION:** The bookends of God's gospel plan reassure us that it will be accomplished, but remind us that we have work to do.

You can download a full transcript of these talks at
WWW.GOSPELSHAPEDCHURCH.ORG/OUTREACH/TALKS

WHAT IS THE GOSPEL PLAN?

* Ask the group members to turn to Session 5 on page 77 of the Handbook. Explain that the diagram on page 79 shows a simple timeline that we will be adding to during this session. (If there might be someone in your group who does not know what "fall" refers to, explain that it refers to the first sin in the Garden of Eden and God's subsequent judgment of mankind.)

GENESIS
THE BOOK OF
BEGINNINGS

REVELATION
THE BOOK
OF ENDINGS

CREATION | FALL | PROMISE

▶ **WATCH DVD 5.1** (5 min 37 sec) **OR DELIVER TALK 5.1** (see page 100)

* Encourage the group to make notes as they watch the DVD or listen to the talk. There is space for notes on page 79 of the Handbook.

Discuss

"The fall had both vertical and horizontal consequences." What evidence is there in your neighborhood that these consequences are still being experienced today?

In the DVD, Erik says: "The vertical consequences are a broken relationship with God, characterized by separation. The horizontal consequences are damaged or broken relationships with others, also characterized by separation." For us today, in our own neighborhood, a "vertical" consequence of sin is that we all die—but this is something we are so used to that we may sometimes forget that death is not "natural." It is the result of the fall. Ask the group to consider what some of the *"horizontal"* consequences are that you see around you in damaged or broken relationships.

☞ GENESIS 3:15

The LORD God said to the serpent: *"I will put enmity between you and the woman, and between your offspring and her offspring; he shall bruise your head, and you shall bruise his heel."*

The gospel was God's plan right from the very beginning. What can we see from the promise in Genesis 3:15 about the "who, what and how" of salvation?

- **Who:** The offspring of the woman.
- **What:** The woman's offspring would destroy the work of the serpent.
- **How:** At great cost! The woman's offspring would also be wounded in the encounter.

Optional question: If you have time, and it would suit your group, you could also ask them: "What other Old Testament events or prophecies do you know that gave further hints about the who, what and how of salvation?"

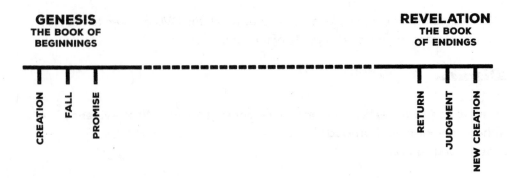

GENESIS
THE BOOK OF
BEGINNINGS

CREATION | FALL | PROMISE

REVELATION
THE BOOK
OF ENDINGS

RETURN | JUDGMENT | NEW CREATION

▶ **WATCH DVD 5.2** (6 min 37 sec) **OR DELIVER TALK 5.2** (see page 100)

✴ *Encourage the group to make notes as they watch the DVD or listen to the talk. There is space for notes on page 80 of the Handbook.*

Discuss

 REVELATION 5:5-6

> *⁵ And one of the elders said to me, "Weep no more; behold, the Lion of the tribe of Judah, the Root of David, has conquered, so that he can open the scroll and its seven seals." ⁶ And between the throne and the four living creatures and among the elders I saw a Lamb standing, as though it had been slain...*

How do the descriptions of Jesus in this passage show us that God's gospel plan has been unfolding throughout history?

- **The Lion of the tribe of Judah:** In Genesis 49, Jacob blesses his sons. In verses 8-10, Judah is compared to a lion—a royal lion, for whom *"the scepter shall not depart … nor the ruler's staff from between his feet, until tribute comes to him; and to him shall be the obedience of the peoples."* In other words, the "Lion of Judah" will be king forever.
- **The Root of David:** Isaiah 11 is a prophecy about the coming Messiah. In it we read that: *"There shall come forth a shoot from the stump of Jesse, and a branch from his roots shall bear fruit. And the Spirit of the Lᴏʀᴅ shall rest upon him"* (v 1-2). This is the "Root of David" (Jesse was David's father).
- **The Lamb that looks as though it has been killed:** In Exodus 12, Passover lambs were sacrificed in place of the firstborn, so that the blood of the lambs protected the people from God's judgment. In John 1:29, Jesus is described as "the Lamb of God, who takes away the sin of the world." But unlike the original lambs, this "Passover Lamb" rose from death. The risen Jesus still had the marks from being crucified (John 20:26-27)—he looked like a lamb who'd been slain—but he will never again die (Hebrews 7:23-28).

The end of God's gospel plan is to gather his redeemed people in the new creation to worship the Lord forever. How should this prospect motivate us for evangelism now?

Being with the Lord forever in the new creation, seeing him face to face and knowing him perfectly, will be far more wonderful than we can imagine (Revelation 21:1-5). We should long for our unsaved family, friends and neighbors to be there too.

103

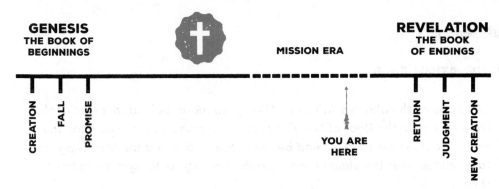

WATCH DVD 5.3 (8 min 32 sec) **OR DELIVER TALK 5.3** (see page 100)

- *Encourage the group to make notes as they watch the DVD or listen to the talk. There is space for notes on page 82 of the Handbook.*

MATTHEW 28:18-20

[18] *"All authority in heaven and on earth has been given to me.* [19] *Go therefore and make disciples of all nations, baptizing them in the name of the Father and of the Son and of the Holy Spirit,* [20] *teaching them to observe all that I have commanded you. And behold, I am with you always, to the end of the age."*

What is our specific job in the "mission era" (see diagram above)?

Making and training disciples. As Erik said, we "talk to people about the gospel. We explain who Jesus is, what he has done, and how we are to respond to him in faith and repentance." We are to make disciples of "all nations"—that means all people groups, ethnicities and countries. We are part of God's great, gospel plan.

When does our job finish?

At "the end of the age." Until the day when Jesus returns, his people will have the exciting privilege and responsibility of sharing the gospel.

"We are not the chef, cooking up the gospel meal; we are simply the waiter, delivering the food to the table."

The gospel plan is God's work that we are privileged to be involved in. How does this liberate us from both inaction and fear?

The gospel plan is God's work, so we can be sure he will carry it out to completion. Why has Jesus not yet come back? Because there are still people waiting to hear the gospel from us, so that they can respond and be converted. What is our main purpose in life, and as a church? It is to be a witness to the saving work of Christ. God's mission in the world needs to be our mission also. Inaction is completely inappropriate.

And fear is also inappropriate. It reveals a lack of trust in God's sovereign hand over our lives. He has called us to be his witnesses, and he will equip us and strengthen us for that task, and use us as we evangelize. Our fears show what we think is truly important. If we fear shame or ridicule, then we are showing that we fear men rather than God.

Ask your group to think again about the two people they have been praying for since Session 1 (page 18 of the Handbook). Have they made an opportunity to talk to them about Jesus yet? If they have, ask them to tell the rest of the group about it as an encouragement to you all. If they haven't, how can the knowledge that the gospel plan is God's work help overcome inaction and fear?

Pray

"Worthy is the Lamb who was slain, to receive power and wealth and wisdom and might and honor and glory and blessing!" **Use these words from Revelation 5:12 to thank and praise Jesus.**

DAILY BIBLE DEVOTIONALS

The daily devotionals this week explore six glimpses of the gospel in the Old Testament, showing how God pointed forward to the life, death, resurrection and rule of his Son, Jesus, throughout his dealings with his Old Testament people. The studies focus on episodes from the lives of Abraham, Moses, David, Naaman and Esther.

SERMONS

OPTION ONE: REVELATION 5:1-14

This is one of the passages Erik looks at in his DVD presentation, which could be expanded upon in a sermon.

OPTION TWO: ACTS 16:11-15

This is part of the passage the Bible study is based on (see next page), which could also be expanded upon in a sermon.

OPTION THREE: ACTS 13:13-43

This passage is not mentioned in this material, but outlines God's plan for his people, as Paul points to the truths that:
- God has always powerfully delivered his people (v 17-20).
- God promised to give his people a King who would save them (v 21-23).
- In Jesus' life, death and resurrection, God has kept all of his promises, fulfilling his great plan of salvation (v 27-33).

If one of your Sunday sermons is to be based on the theme of this session, church members will find a page to write notes on the sermon on page 91 of their Handbooks.

BIBLE STUDY

AIM: The main teaching session this week laid out how the gospel was God's plan from the very beginning, and where the plan will finish. The daily readings illustrated how the gospel plan unfolded throughout the Bible. This Bible-study session aims to get group members clear about God's part and our part in evangelism, and to see how God's gospel is for everyone.

Discuss

Have you ever been involved in organizing something where it has not been clear who was in charge and what specific roles people were playing? What happened? What lessons were learned?

> The aim here is to draw out the chaos and upset that ensues when people don't know what they are doing, and the resentment it causes when people start doing a job that someone else thinks is their role. Try to have fun with this question rather than make it weighty!

 READ ACTS 16:11-34

1. What evangelistic strategy did Paul and Silas have (v 13)? In what other ways and in what other places did God use them while they were in Philippi (v 16-18, 23-30)?

> Usually they went to the synagogue and preached about Christ from the Scriptures. But at Philippi, they went down to the river, which was a local place of prayer, perhaps because there was no synagogue. They may have been pursuing a "low-hanging fruit" strategy—speaking to people who already knew something about the God of the Bible, and the promises of the Messiah.

> Through circumstance, God put them in a position where the gospel reached two rather unlikely people. It looks as if they only preached to the slave girl out of annoyance (v 18). Their subsequent imprisonment then led to an amazing gospel opportunity.

2. **What kinds of people became the first Christians in Philippi? Can you think of modern parallels to the different kinds of people that responded to the gospel?**

  - **Lydia.** A wealthy foreign businesswoman who was a "God-fearer"—a Gentile who respected and worshiped the God of the Bible.
  - **Her household.** Presumably family and servants.
  - **A possessed slave girl.** Who was owned and used as a fortuneteller by her owners to make money.
  - **The jailer.** A tough hard man, probably a retired soldier from the Roman army.
  - **His household.** Presumably including family of all ages.

3. **What was the order of events in the conversion of Lydia? Who did what?**

  - **Paul and Silas preached the Gospel!** They started to tell people about Jesus.
  - **The Lord opened Lydia's heart.** He enabled her to respond to the message.
  - **Lydia shared the message with her household**, and they were all baptized.
  - **Lydia opened her home to Paul and Silas.** Her response to the message leads her to be a generous supporter of the gospel mission by giving hospitality to the evangelists.

  Many commentators have talked about three "openings." The apostles opened their mouths; the Lord opened Lydia's heart; Lydia opened her home.

4. **What happens to our witness if we forget that:**

  - **it is God's work to open people's hearts and minds to the gospel?**

  If we think it is our part to do the whole thing we will be crushed by the responsibility, and be consumed with guilt and anxiety about our gospel witness. We will also be tempted to twist the gospel, or use manipulative techniques in order to get a "result." See 2 Corinthians 4:1-3.

  - **God does his work as his people open their mouths and proclaim the gospel?**

  If we think it is God's part to do the whole thing, we will never bother to reach out with the gospel to others. This is disastrous. It leads to Christians who are completely cut off from non-Christians, and churches that are focused on themselves. When we lose a focus on outreach, we will tend to argue and fragment over smaller and smaller doctrinal matters.

5. So what counts as success in evangelism? What counts as failure?

Success=faithfulness in telling others, not some arbitrary view of results or decisions. Evangelist Rico Tice comments: *"Our job is not to convert people. It is to witness to Christ. Conversion isn't the mark of a successful witness— witnessing is. Think about a courtroom. Witnesses are there to tell the truth. That's successful witness. If the jury don't believe them, that's not their fault or their failure. You have not failed if you explain the gospel and are rejected. You have failed if you don't try."*

How does this understanding of both God's part and our part in outreach liberate us to be more active and bold in evangelism?

We just have to tell the gospel. We can trust God to do his work, and we are privileged to be part of his great plan of reconciliation in the world. This is massively liberating.

6. What are the biggest reasons why we don't share the gospel more with other people?

Although this is phrased as a general question, it is an opportunity for you to find out where people are struggling personally. Some people may say "Laziness" —but do not accept this as an answer! It is not laziness, but pride, selfishness or a lack of love or belief in the gospel.

How does the experience of Paul and Silas in evangelism in this passage help us with these? Try to give specific examples of how this might work in your life.

- **We fear rejection and "persecution".** The kind of rejection we face is far smaller than that faced by Paul, Silas and many of our brothers and sisters in other parts of the world. In fact, the promise is that the Christian life will necessarily involve rejection and persecution, so we should just "man (or woman) up."

- **We don't know any people to share the gospel with.** This can be alarmingly true for many church people whose lives are built around relationships with other Christians and church events. Paul and Silas made specific plans to meet with people who might be open to listen. They planned for it. They also made use of opportunities in the course of daily life. And they used their life circumstances to testify to Christ. We can do all these things.
- **We don't know the gospel.** It's not that hard in outline (v 31)—but we do need to train ourselves.
- **We can be fearful about what will happen to us.** Paul and Silas were able to rejoice in their "difficult" circumstances—singing songs in prison. But this was because they were confident in the sovereignty of God over their circumstances, and that God was working out the gospel plan in and through them.
- **We can assume that some people will simply not be interested in the gospel.** We can unconsciously "filter out" some people as unresponsive for cultural, religious or ideological reasons. But the gospel is for everyone with a pulse. The slave girl and the jailer would not be high on anyone's list of "people most likely to get converted," and yet they were the people God chose to reach out to. Notice that Paul seems to evangelize the slave girl out of annoyance more than anything else!
- **We can be fearful about where it will lead.** Sometimes we fail to start talking with "difficult people" because we are concerned that there will be a high relational cost for us in the future. We don't want to start something we will find hard to finish. But God brings people into his church—a fellowship of love and care. Those he calls, he also protects and equips for service. God will do his work in them, and we need not fear that he will leave it undone.

7. **Imagine going to a meeting of the church in Philippi shortly after the events in this chapter. Who would be in the congregation? What kinds of unbelievers might also have been present? How does this showcase God's gospel plan?**

A wealthy businesswoman, a previously possessed slave girl, and a tough jailer (possibly an ex-soldier) and his family. God's gospel plan is to rescue sinners from every nation, tribe and race by his grace.

How might remembering God's gospel plan to call all kinds of people change the way we think about outreach?

We can become a bit monochrome in our evangelistic imagination—just going for people and people groups that we think are "low-hanging fruit," and never considering others. The gospel is for everyone with a pulse. We should be open for whatever opportunities come our way as we pray for them. We need to keep speaking so that they may hear the good news and respond. God is with us in our efforts to reach out with the gospel.

Apply

FOR YOURSELF: What difference will knowing both your part and God's part in evangelism make to you this week?

FOR YOUR CHURCH: To what extent are you genuinely showing in your congregation that God's gospel plan is to call people from every nation and every stratum of society? What can you do differently to make sure you are not unhelpfully discriminating in your outreach?

Note that some churches cannot help but be more "monochrome" culturally, because of the area they are placed in. But even so, church families should be mixing across generations as well as other cultural divides. Use this question to ask if there are ways that we are deliberately "self selecting" the kind of people that we meet with in an unhelpful way.

Pray

Think about the two people you have been praying for. And then pray that God would do his work of opening their hearts as you speak the gospel.

FOR YOURSELF: Pray that you would understand that God calls us just to speak, and that you would rejoice in the work God is doing in the world.

FOR YOUR WHOLE CHURCH: Pray that you would grow in boldness to reach out with the gospel to everyone and anyone.

FURTHER READING

The Spirit of Christ is the Spirit of missions. The nearer we get to him, the more intensely missionary we become.
Henry Martyn

There is not a better evangelist in the world than the Holy Spirit.
D.L. Moody

Books

- *The Scriptures Testify about Me: Jesus and the Gospel in the Old Testament* (ed. Don Carson)
- *God's Big Picture (Vaughan Roberts)*
- *The Big Story (Justin Buzzard)*

Online

- *Christ is not Just Another Theme in the Old Testament:* gospelshapedchurch. org/resources251
- *Don't you Know Jesus is Real?* gospelshapedchurch.org/resources252

LEADER'S REFLECTIONS

SESSION 6:

HOW SHOULD WE PRAY?

"EFFECTIVE EVANGELISM BEGINS WITH PERSEVERING PRAYER," WROTE THE ENGLISH PASTOR DICK LUCAS. WE MUST REACH UP TO GOD IF WE ARE TO REACH OUT TO PEOPLE. IN THIS SESSION, WE WILL CONSIDER WHY PRAYER IS SO VITAL, AND WHAT THE CONTENT OF OUR PRAYING ABOUT WITNESS SHOULD BE.

TALK OUTLINE

6.1 ● We're in a spiritual battle, but we do not fight alone. Prayer connects us with the unlimited resources of our heavenly Father. But how do we pray for evangelism?

● **PRAY FOR LABORERS** *Matthew 9:35-38*
  • We often think the harvest is puny and the workers abound; but Jesus taught the opposite. Be encouraged!
  • We need to pray for more workers, and that workers will be focused on reaching the lost.

● **PRAY FOR OPPORTUNITIES** *Colossians 4:2-4*
  • Paul isn't naturally bold; he's supernaturally bold.
  • We're locked outside of the human heart; we pray that God will open a door for the gospel.
  • *Share an example of how God has answered your prayers for opportunities.*
  • If you are interested in buying something (a car, item of clothing, gadget, etc.), you start noticing them everywhere. *(Share an example from your own life.)* When we pray for opportunities, we start seeing them.

6.2 ● **PRAY FOR FAITHFULNESS** *Ephesians 6:18-20*
  • Paul prays that he would take opportunities; the purpose of an open door is to walk through it.
  • Paul prays for faithfulness—clarity and boldness in speaking the message.
  • When we fear God more than man, we are bold.

● **PRAY FOR BLESSING**
  • Paul prays for the gospel to advance as people are converted.
  • It's ignorant and arrogant to bemoan the condition of society or talk about revival without praying for it.

● **CONCLUSION:** Prayer fuels mission. Pray for laborers, opportunities, faithfulness, boldness and blessing—and then watch what God does!

 You can download a full transcript of these talks at
WWW.GOSPELSHAPEDCHURCH.ORG/OUTREACH/TALKS

HOW SHOULD WE PRAY?

* *Ask the group members to turn to Session 6 on page 93 of the Handbook.*

Discuss

Have you ever prayed for an opportunity to talk about Jesus to someone? What happened?

When we actually pray for opportunities to talk about God, he tends to give them (though not necessarily in the way we might have expected or hoped for). But we find it easy to forget this. Hopefully, some of your group will have prayed for an opportunity, and then have been given one, though do be prepared with an example from your own life.

If you do give an example yourself, make sure it is not triumphalistic. In this session we will be thinking about not just praying for opportunities, but also the courage required to take them and the need for the answer we give to be clear. You might give an example where there was an opportunity you failed to take, or one which you did take and messed up in some way.

NOTE: If no one has prayed and been given a gospel opportunity, then move on to the DVD, explaining that this session is going to help us to know why and what to pray.

▶ **WATCH DVD 6.1** (5 min 39 sec) **OR DELIVER TALK 6.1** (see page 116)

* *Encourage the group to make notes as they watch the DVD or listen to the talk. There is space for notes on page 95 of the Handbook.*

Discuss

 **MATTHEW 9:37-38**

> *³⁷ Then he said to his disciples, "The harvest is plentiful, but the laborers are few; ³⁸ therefore pray earnestly to the Lord of the harvest to send out laborers into his harvest."*

Erik said: *"We tend to think that the harvest is puny and the workers abound."* Why do we think this?

Answers will reflect the church the group are from and the nature of the surrounding neighborhood. They might include:

- We don't have many friendships or contact much with non-believers, so we don't see the true size of the potential harvest.
- We may see lots of churches around, and therefore assume that there are plenty of workers.
- We may have very active programs at our own church, and therefore think we have already provided enough workers.

What would change for us if we really believed the opposite?

- We would "pray earnestly" for more workers, and do so regularly.
- We would pray that our workers really work—not just taking opportunities that may arise, but actively making opportunities to share the gospel.
- We would look for and see more opportunities around us. (You could link this with the "white van" example from the DVD. Just as a person thinking of buying a white van suddenly notices them everywhere, so someone actively praying for evangelistic opportunities will see them popping up around them.)

***"The human heart is a formidable mountain, unable to be opened by any amount of human exertion."* How is this both a challenge and an encouragement to us?**

It is a challenge because, no matter how carefully we prepare or how eloquent our words, we know that won't be enough to open someone's heart to hear the truth of the gospel message.

It is an encouragement because it makes us rely on God. It is only through the Holy Spirit that a non-believer's heart can be opened (Acts 16:14).

Pray

We want to model praying for evangelism in this session, not just talking about it! So, we have included suggestions for your group to pray in each discussion break. Encourage them to pray in groups of three or four; and to make sure they spend more time praying than talking about what to pray for!

"Prayer connects us with the unlimited resources of our Father in heaven."

Thank God that there is a ripe harvest, and pray for workers to go into the harvest field of:
- **your family**
- **your neighborhood**
- **your workplace**

Pray that your church will be a missionary family that is reaching out to the area it is situated in.

"Lord, give me an opportunity to tell some else about the gospel today—and please don't be subtle!" **Why not pray this prayer for each other now?**

▶ **WATCH DVD 6.2** (3 min 53 sec) **OR DELIVER TALK 6.2** (see page 116)

✱ *Encourage the group to make notes as they watch the DVD or listen to the talk. There is space for notes on page 97 of the Handbook.*

Discuss

☞ **EPHESIANS 6:18-20**

[18] ... making supplication for all the saints, [19] and also for me, that words may be given to me in opening my mouth boldly to proclaim the mystery of the gospel, [20] for which I am an ambassador in chains, that I may declare it boldly, as I ought to speak.

In Session 1, we saw from this passage that Paul asked people to pray for words and for boldness. Have you been praying for boldness for yourself and others? If you have, what has happened? If you haven't, why not?

If group members have been praying for boldness since Session 1, and asking others to do so as well (see page 18 of the Handbook), you can be sure God has been answering those prayers. So this is a great opportunity to encourage one another as you hear what God has been doing. If there have been clear answers to prayer, rejoice in these together.

But bear in mind that you may have one or more people in your group who have never before spoken to a non-believer about Christ. For them, the smallest conversation about Jesus is still a huge step and a fantastic answer to prayer. So it's worth being careful that the group doesn't get overly excited about "big" answers (eg: "My friend fell on his knees right away and gave his life to Jesus") rather than seemingly "smaller" ones (eg: "My neighbor said she'd think about coming to the Christmas service").

If some of the group have *not* been praying for boldness, ask them why not. Then see if there's something practical you can put in place so that every group member prays for boldness and faithfulness this week. For example, could someone in the group commit to texting/emailing the others at a set time each day to remind them to pray? Arrange to talk about this again next week to see how things are going.

"Imagine what would happen in your life, your church family and your city if you and other believers started praying like a missionary."
What do you imagine might happen?

We started to think about this in Session 3, when we considered that the church is like a missionary family (pages 47-51). If the group is finding it hard to imagine what difference praying like a missionary might make, look at their answers in Session 3 for a helpful starting point.

What practical changes can you make so that you don't just *imagine* praying like a missionary, but it begins to happen in reality?

Hopefully the group has already started doing this:
- In Session 1, they were asked to think of two people they want to share the

gospel with, and to start praying for them.
- In Session 3 Bible Study (and again, above), they were asked to pray for boldness, both for themselves and for others.

In addition to these, encourage the group to think of ways, times and places in which they can encourage each other to keep praying, eg:
- at church on a Sunday
- in a midweek group
- as part of daily devotionals
- using social media
- meeting with a prayer partner

Pray

Spend some time in prayer for each other and your church as a whole:
- **Pray for faithfulness.**
- **Pray for boldness.**
- **Pray for blessing.**

DAILY BIBLE DEVOTIONALS

This week's individual devotional studies focus in detail on one of the passages Erik speaks about in his talk—Colossians 4:2-6. We'll see how Paul emphasizes the need for our prayers, our words and our lifestyles each to be committed to sharing the gospel.

SERMONS

OPTION ONE: EPHESIANS 6:13-20

This passage includes some verses that Erik looks at in his DVD presentation (v 18-20), which could be expanded upon in a sermon.

OPTION TWO: 1 TIMOTHY 2:1-7

This is the passage the Bible study is based on (see next page), which could also be expanded upon in a sermon.

OPTION THREE: MATTHEW 6:7-15

The Lord's Prayer is not mentioned in this material, but picks up on several of the themes of this session, especially:
- Our position in prayer: as children, speaking to our all-powerful Father (v 9).
- Our priority in prayer: for God's name to be honored and his kingdom to come (v 9-10).
- Our petition in prayer: for both physical and spiritual needs, acknowledging that we rely on our Father for all things (v 11-13).

If one of your Sunday sermons is to be based on the theme of this session, church members will find a page to write notes on the sermon on page 107 of their Handbooks.

BIBLE STUDY

AIM: The main teaching session this week encouraged us to pray for workers, opportunities, boldness, clarity and blessing. The daily readings underline and illustrate these points from Colossians 4. This Bible-study session aims to get group members to understand that when we pray for our evangelism as individuals and as a church, we are praying within the will of God; we are asking him to do the very thing he has told and shown us he wants to do in the world.

Discuss

Think back to when you were a child. What particular things did you do that particularly pleased your parents or teachers? Why were they pleased with these things? What effect did that have on you?

Most parents will be pleased when children are polite, tidy, obedient and work hard at things. It's because our parents love us and want to give us habits that will help us do well in life. But some parents can unhelpfully only be pleased at success, rather than effort. When pleasure is communicated well—ie: by praise and compliments—it can powerfully encourage us to work harder at pleasing people. We can also be discouraged by aloofness or lack of recognition.

 READ 1 TIMOTHY 2:1-7

> *¹ First of all, then, I urge that supplications, prayers, intercessions, and thanksgivings be made for all people...*

1. What, does Paul tell us, pleases God (v 1-3)? What does God desire (v 4)?

He wants us to pray—for all people, but particularly for those in authority and leadership. It pleases God that we pray with thanksgiving. Verses 3-4 tell us that God desires that all people be saved.

NOTE: Christians have struggled to reconcile the two truths that God desires "all people" to be saved (see Ezekiel 18:23), and that God chooses and effectually calls only some (see Romans 8:29-30). There have been various attempts to harmonize these views. Calvin and others have thought that "all people" must be viewed as "people from every nation and class of society" (see verse 7). Both truths are taught explicitly in the Bible. John Stott comments: *"The right response is neither to seek a superficial harmonization ... nor to declare that Jesus and Paul are contradicting themselves, but to affirm that both are true while humbly confessing that at present our little minds are unable to resolve it"* (The Message of 1 Timothy & Titus).

2. Who are we to pray for?

All people—because God wants all people to be saved. *"The gospel is for anyone with a pulse!"* That means all kinds of people, of all races, nations, statuses and conditions. We are also to pray especially for those in high positions.

NOTE: Your group may be tempted to ask what the difference is between the different kinds of prayer mentioned—supplications, prayers, intercessions and thanksgiving. Thanksgiving is easy to understand. It's possible to see different nuances between supplication, prayers and intercession, but that's not the big point. The list urges us to pour ourselves out in prayer for the conditions to spread the gospel, and for the salvation of people—it is that important. And importantly, we are to be thankful for our leaders—whether we voted for them or not!

What is the purpose of praying for all those "in high positions" (v 2, 4)?

We are to pray that they would rule us in such a way that we are able to lead a peaceful, quiet life that is godly and dignified in every way (v 2). But the reason we are to ask this is so that we would have an open door to be able to share the gospel with others. The *Pax Romana* (the peace that existed under Roman rule over much of Europe) was a major factor in the early spread of the gospel message.

Additional question: Why is it easier to just pray v 2, without the reason of v 4?

We would love a quiet life on its own. But we pray for a quiet life for a purpose—the purpose of being free to spread the message about Jesus.

3. **How is God described in these verses? How does this help us see the priority of evangelism for Christians and churches?**

- *God our Savior (v 3):* God is in the business of saving people. His plan for the world is a salvation plan—that is the story we are part of.
- *God desires that people be saved and know the truth (v 4):* we should desire the same things.
- *There is one God (v 5):* all other gods are false gods—we should urge people to worship the one true God.
- *God appoints and sends preachers (v 7):* he communicates his message of salvation through human agents.

4. **What are some of the reasons why we fail to pray for the gospel to advance?**

- We think that God may not be that interested in some people.
- We might not be bothered that other people live with their idols. Have we swallowed the lie of our culture, that it doesn't matter what you believe so long as you are sincere?
- We are fearful that our prayers will not be answered.

How do these truths about God encourage us to pray?

- We are asking God to help us do the very thing that he wants to do! We are praying in his will. We know that God delights to give good things to his children, so it should encourage us.
- The gospel is true. It is the truth that sets us free. But only God can open blind eyes to the truth, so we need to ask him to do it.

5. **How is Christ described in verses 5-6? How does that help us with the content of what our message should be?**

- *Jesus is a Mediator:* we need Christ to bring us to God, from whom we are by nature estranged. See also Hebrews 9:13-15.
- *He is a man:* he became incarnate to reveal the truth about God and to die in our place. See also Romans 1:3; Hebrews 2:14, 17-18.
- *He gave himself as a ransom:* our slavery to sin requires a price to be paid. Jesus was prepared to pay that price with his own life. See also Mark 10:45; Titus 2:14.

- *Jesus is the testimony at the proper time:* his coming, death and resurrection were promised in the Old Testament. He tells us and shows us the truth about God. See also Galatians 4:4; Hebrews 1:1-2.

6. How do these truths about Jesus encourage us to pray?

God has done the hard part in salvation. People need a mediator, which God has provided. People need rescuing from slavery: God has provided a ransom. People need to hear the truth: God has spoken clearly and finally in Jesus. We should pray out of gratitude for what God has done for us. We should pray because we love the lost, as God does. We should pray because people need Jesus to rescue them.

Apply

FOR YOURSELF: Who do you find it hardest to pray for and why? How can you help yourself to be more consistent and persistent with your prayers for others to find Christ?

We find it hard to pray for:
- those for whom we have prayed over a long time.
- people who have disappointed/hurt us.
- those who seem hardened to the gospel.
- those we just cannot imagine will ever become Christians.

We can help by getting ourselves organized and using a prayer journal or a system that reminds us to pray. Prayer triplets or partnerships can also help.

FOR YOUR GROUP: How can you encourage each other to pray, not just for health problems or other life difficulties, but also for more proactive evangelism?

Encourage people to share someone to pray for each week, and not just list ailments! You might also ask in a small-group context for ideas on how to approach people you know, and for things that you might say to them in answer to specific questions they may have. Many people have found that being part of a prayer triplet or partnership can be very helpful in keeping focused on the work of evangelism.

FOR YOUR CHURCH: What opportunities are there for us to pray together for our outreach as a whole church? How can we keep prayer for outreach high up the agenda?

For formal prayer meetings, it is important that the church keeps focused on prayer for gospel outreach around the world, but especially in your local area. You should discuss whether and how it might be important to pray for outreach in your regular Sunday meetings. What effect might such prayers have on non-believers who are present, if they are badly or inappropriately expressed? What is a good way to pray for the work of the gospel at a meeting where non-Christians might be present?

Pray

Pray again for the people you requested prayer for last week. Share any news for thanksgiving and encouragement. How has God answered your prayers from last week?

FOR YOUR WHOLE CHURCH: Pray that you would become a church dedicated to praying to the Lord of the harvest for him to work through you to bring "all people" under the sound of the only gospel that can save them.

FURTHER READING

> Until the gate of hell is shut upon a man, we must not cease to pray for him. And if we see him hugging the very doorposts of damnation, we must go to the mercy seat and beseech the arm of grace to pluck him from his dangerous position. While there is life there is hope.
>
> **C.H. Spurgeon**

> Work as if everything depended on you. Pray as if everything depended on God.
>
> **Augustine**

Books

- *The Best-Kept Secret of Christian Mission, chapter 4 (John Dickson)*
- *A Praying Life (Paul Miller)*
- *Operation World: The Definitive Prayer Guide to Every Nation (Jason Mandryk)*

Online

- *What if I'm not a Gifted Evangelist?*
  gospelshapedchurch.org/resources261

LEADER'S REFLECTIONS

SESSION 7:

WHAT DO WE SAY?

IF WE ARE PRAYING FOR OPPORTUNITIES AND LOOKING
FOR OPPORTUNITIES TO SHARE THE GOSPEL, THEN WE
WILL FIND OURSELVES IN POSITIONS WHERE WE ARE
ABLE TO TALK ABOUT THE GOSPEL. BUT... WHAT DO WE
ACTUALLY SAY? WHAT ARE THE THINGS WE MUST AIM
TO TALK ABOUT, AND HOW DO WE SPEAK ABOUT THE
GOSPEL IN WAYS THAT MAKE SENSE AND RESONATE WITH
THOSE WE'RE SPEAKING TO? THOSE ARE THE QUESTIONS
WE WILL CONSIDER IN THE NEXT TWO SESSIONS.

TALK OUTLINE

7.1 • *Share an example of someone who avoids evangelizing for fear of failure.* Effective evangelism is not dependent on our intelligence or skill; it's the faithful proclamation of the gospel.

● **THE GOSPEL IS THE GOOD NEWS ABOUT WHAT JESUS HAS DONE**
1 Corinthians 15:1-8
The gospel is a **message** that must be preached and received.

● **THE GOSPEL IS NOT WHAT WE HAVE DONE FOR GOD BUT WHAT GOD HAS DONE FOR US** *Romans 10:17*
The gospel is *not* about our experiences or our life—it's about Christ's experiences and life. And it is *not* something that is happening now—it's something that happened in the past. The the gospel is Jesus.

● **THE GOSPEL IS THE GOOD NEWS ABOUT WHAT GOD HAS DONE WITH OUR SIN** *2 Corinthians 5:21*
• Christ died **for** our sins.
• *Share a story of someone realizing the weight of their sin and/or the wonder of Christ's sacrificial, sin-bearing death for the first time.*
• Our sin means that we are guilty, and have earned God's wrath. Jesus suffered what his people deserve so that we could receive what Jesus earned.

● **THE GOSPEL IS HISTORICAL** *1 Corinthians 15:5-8*
We should press home the historical truth of the gospel.

● **THE GOSPEL IS TO BE BELIEVED**
Faithful evangelism urges people to respond in **repentance** and **faith**; to change their minds about who Jesus is, go his way and trust in his cross.

● **CONCLUSION:** God-honoring evangelism is faithfully communicating the truth of the gospel. Let's talk about what Jesus has done.

You can download a full transcript of this talk at
WWW.GOSPELSHAPEDCHURCH.ORG/OUTREACH/TALKS

WHAT DO WE SAY?

* *Ask the group members to turn to Session 7 on page 109 of the Handbook.*

Discuss

Have you ever learned or used a gospel outline (The Bridge to Life, The Roman Road, The Wordless Book, Two Ways to Live, etc.)? What do you think was good about it? Was there anything that was not so good?

The aim here isn't to champion a particular gospel outline, or to criticize any of them, but simply briefly to begin to discuss how such outlines can/cannot help us. Don't worry if your group isn't familiar with any/all of these outlines; just move on to the DVD.

WATCH DVD 7.1 (14 min 14 sec) **OR LISTEN TO TALK 7.1** (see page 132)

* *There is a note on page 111 of the Handbook that says:* **"In this session, we're thinking about how we explain the gospel to others. As you watch the DVD or listen to the talk, make a note of any phrases or ideas that you personally might find helpful when sharing the gospel."**

* *Encourage the group to do this as they watch the DVD or listen to the talk.*

1 CORINTHIANS 15:1-8

¹ *Now I would remind you, brothers, of the gospel I preached to you, which you received, in which you stand,* ² *and by which you are being saved, if you hold fast to the word I preached to you—unless you believed in vain.*

³ *For I delivered to you as of first importance what I also received: that Christ died for our sins in accordance with the Scriptures,* ⁴ *that he was buried, that he was raised on the third day in accordance with the Scriptures,* ⁵ *and that he appeared to Cephas, then to the twelve.* ⁶ *Then he appeared to more than five hundred brothers at one time, most of whom are still alive,*

though some have fallen asleep. ⁷ Then he appeared to James, then to all the apostles. ⁸ Last of all, as to one untimely born, he appeared also to me.

𝒟𝒾𝓈𝒸𝓊𝓈𝓈

In 1 Corinthians 15, Paul is reminding the Christians in Corinth about the message he shared with them. What does he tell us about the gospel in verses 1 and 2?

- The gospel must be preached/proclaimed.
- It must be received and held fast to ie: believed as well as understood.
- It is the way to be saved.
- It is of first importance.

The word "gospel" means "good news." The gospel message is the good news about Jesus. Underline the things we learn about Jesus in verses 3-8.

> ³ For I delivered to you as of first importance what I also received: that **Christ died for our sins** in **accordance with the Scriptures**, ⁴ that he was **buried**, that he was **raised on the third day** in **accordance with the Scriptures**, ⁵ and that he **appeared** to Cephas, then to the twelve. ⁶ Then he appeared to more than five hundred brothers at one time, most of whom are still alive, though some have fallen asleep. ⁷ Then he appeared to James, then to all the apostles. ⁸ Last of all, as to one untimely born, he appeared also to me.

Paul says that delivering the message about Jesus is "of first importance" (v 3). How would you tell someone the good news about Jesus in just one minute? Use the words and phrases you underlined to help you.

It is very easy to make the gospel sound complex, and far harder to explain it simply, in language someone unfamiliar with the Bible can understand! Most of us find it harder than we expect to explain the whole gospel in a simple way, in a single minute. If you have time, divide your group into pairs and ask them to explain the gospel to each other in turn, and then offer feedback on each other's efforts.

The key words and phrases to use are as follows. There's a further explanation in brackets.

- Jesus is the Christ (ie: God's promised, chosen, eternal King).
- He died (by being executed on a cross) and was buried (he was definitely dead).
- He died for our sins—to take the punishment for our rebellion against God, which displays itself in our actions, thoughts and words that disobey him—our "sins."
- God had promised many hundreds of years previously that he would send his chosen King to save his people. These promises are written in the Old Testament ("the Scriptures").
- Jesus didn't stay dead but was raised to life. (This happened "on the third day," ie: Jesus died on the Friday, the "first" day, and rose again on the Sunday, the "third" day.)
- The risen Jesus was seen by hundreds of people, including those who knew him well (eg: Peter, called "Cephas" here, and James); to huge crowds ("five hundred brothers at one time"); and to Paul (the writer of 1 Corinthians).

What do you think people would find weird from your explanation?

The main purpose of this question and the following one is to help group members think about how the gospel message may sound to people in your area, particularly if they have no biblical or Christian knowledge.

Almost any part of the message about Jesus might sound weird to someone listening to it for the first time, but the reasons may differ. They may find it hard to believe the historical accuracy of what they are hearing; or to grasp the concept of sin and the need for it to be punished; or to accept that one man's death can pay the price for many people.

Would they have found anything offensive?

At its heart, the gospel message is offensive because it says that people are helpless and hopeless without Jesus. There is absolutely nothing they can do to earn or deserve salvation. They have to admit this in order to accept God's grace.

Some may also be offended at being asked to believe something that seems to them to be unbelievable (eg: "Dead bodies don't come back to life"; "A man who lived 2000 years ago can't have any relevance to my life").

How might you start to unpack some of those weird or offensive ideas in a way that is helpful for them?

This will vary according to the background of the unbeliever. For example, some will find it helpful to examine the evidence for the accuracy of the biblical documents. Others may be helped more by hearing how the gospel has made a difference in the life of a believer. Some people are satisfied with short, simple answers, while others may want to read more fully about a particular topic or concept. You may want to suggest some short, clear books that address some of the issues that unbelievers struggle with—see page 144 for a list.

If someone is offended by the concept of grace and the idea that salvation is a gift that cannot be earned, it may help to explain the reassurance that comes from knowing that our right relationship with God is based on what *Jesus* has done, not on what *we* do. As a Christian, I can be confident that my future is secure because there's nothing I can do to spoil that, as long as I "hold fast" to the gospel of Jesus Christ. But if salvation was dependent on my own ability to live in a particular way or keep special rules, I would live under constant fear of messing it up and losing out. There is great joy and reassurance in a gospel of grace.

Life does not always offer us an opportunity to say everything about the gospel. What advantages and pitfalls are there in communicating only part of the gospel message in a conversation?

When we have an opportunity to explain the whole of the Christian message, we should try to give an overview of the main points of the gospel. We mustn't miss out parts we think may be unpalatable if we have opportunity to talk about them.

But if our opportunity is only brief, it is not wrong to make just one or two simple points—for example, speaking about Jesus' resurrection without speaking about his death, or *vice versa*, depending on the circumstances and topic of conversation.

If time or opportunity is short, we can make a single, impactful point really well, while bearing in mind that we have not said *everything* by making a single point.

Always try to connect what you say to Jesus, eg: not "I believe that God is love" but "I believe that God is love because Jesus' life/death/resurrection showed it."

If time is short, it is always a good idea to finish by saying: "I'd love to share more of what I believe about Jesus with you. Would you like to talk about it another time when we have a little longer?"

Set aside some time this week to practice your quick explanation of the gospel. When will you do that?

Encourage people to write down an actual time in their Handbook or (better) their calendar.

Pray

Look again at the words and phrases you underlined in verses 3-8. Thank and praise Jesus for each of these truths about him.

Ask God to help you refine your explanation of the gospel as you practice it this week.

Continue to pray for the people you want to share the gospel with.

DAILY BIBLE DEVOTIONALS

These studies look at six instances of gospel communication in the Gospels and the book of Acts. They show how the content of the gospel is unchanging, but that the way it is proclaimed varies according to the context and the person/people receiving the message.

SERMONS

OPTION ONE: 1 CORINTHIANS 15:1-11

This is the passage Erik bases his DVD presentation on, which could be expanded upon in a sermon.

OPTION TWO: ACTS 10:1-3, 34-44

This is the passage the Bible study is based on (see next page), which could also be expanded upon in a sermon.

OPTION THREE: ROMANS 3:21-26

This passage is not mentioned in this material, but picks up on several of the themes of this session, as it outlines the gospel message:
- We are made right with God by faith in Jesus Christ—and can only be made right with him in this way (v 21-22).
- This is because we are all sinful, having fallen short of God's purpose for us and his commands to us (v 23).
- Righteousness is available because Jesus died to bear God's just wrath in our place, so that we could be found innocent by God (v 24-26).

If one of your Sunday sermons is to be based on the theme of this session, church members will find a page to write notes on the sermon on page 123 of their Handbooks.

BIBLE STUDY

AIM: The main teaching session this week showed how our message must be focused on speaking about Jesus. This Bible study aims to cement that understanding, and to help the group start to think more clearly about how it might express these essential gospel truths in ways that are relevant and understandable in our culture.

Discuss

Have you ever had a culinary disaster when making a cake or following a complicated recipe? What went wrong?

> Just to get people talking about the consequences when you miss out some ingredient from a recipe. The gospel message's elements are not like different parts of a meal, where (for instance), if you leave out potatoes, the rest of the meal is unaffected. The gospel is like a cake, where, if you leave out a vital ingredient, the whole thing stops being "cake" and becomes something else.

 READ ACTS 10:1-3; 34-44

> ¹ *At Caesarea there was a man named Cornelius, a centurion of what was known as the Italian Cohort,* ² *a devout man who feared God with all his household, gave alms generously to the people, and prayed continually to God...*

* *If you have time, you might get the group to speed read the whole chapter before focusing in on Peter's message.*

Up to this point in the book of Acts, only Jews and Samaritans have become followers of Jesus. Despite the promise of Acts 1:8 ("*you will be my witnesses in Jerusalem and in all Judea and Samaria, and to the ends of the earth...*"), it was not yet clear to the apostles that the gospel was also for the Gentiles. After God gives a vision to Cornelius to send for Peter (10:1-7), Peter (verses 9-17) is told to go to preach the message to Cornelius, and his Gentile friends.

1. How is Cornelius described (see verses 1-2)?

He is a God-fearing Gentile—probably a Roman—who is devout, fears God along with his household, is a generous donor to the poor, and has a rich prayer life.

What is he missing (see also verses 43-44)?

He knows about the God of the Bible, and has responded as he is able to, but he has not received the Holy Spirit (v 44), because he has not believed the gospel of forgiveness (v 43—it is as we repent and trust Christ that we receive his Spirit, see Acts 2:38). So Cornelius is religious, but not saved.

2. What is the content of the message Peter speaks to these Gentiles? List the elements, and explain what they mean.

- *God is the God of the whole world,* and this message is for everyone (v 34-35).
- *Jesus Christ is Lord of all* (v 36).
- *Jesus was a human* who preached and showed he was from God by his miracles, character and power over evil forces.
- *Jesus died.* "Hanging on a tree" (v 39) is a biblical picture that is pregnant with meaning—ie: he was cursed by God in our place (see Deuteronomy 21:23; 1 Peter 2:24).
- *God raised Jesus to life.*
- *The apostles are witnesses to this.* The language makes it clear that this is an historical event, attested to by many, many people.
- *Jesus is the coming judge of all people (v 42).* God has appointed him to be judge of the living and the dead.
- *Through Jesus we are offered forgiveness of our sins (v 43).* This is a gift.
- *Our response is to "believe in him" (v 43);* that is, to believe in both who he is (Lord), which implies repentance, and what he has done (died so we might be forgiven). We receive forgiveness as we put our trust in him— which means to submit to his rule as Lord, and rely on his death for our forgiveness.

3. What might he have had to say differently if Cornelius had never heard about Jesus; or if Cornelius had been a devout worshiper of Zeus, instead of the God of the Bible?

He would need to have gone into much greater detail about Jesus' life, death and resurrection. It would have taken a long time for Cornelius to understand the significance of who Jesus was and is.

If Cornelius has been a Zeus worshiper, Peter might have had to spend longer talking about the character and nature of the one true God, perhaps by showing them how the character and works of Jesus revealed him.

4. **How does this observation help us in understanding our role as a messenger of the good news about Jesus? What do we constantly need to work at? What did Peter do (v 29)?**

Although the content of our message will remain the same, different parts will need emphasizing or explaining carefully, depending on the person who is hearing it. We therefore need to work at both understanding our hearers, and thinking about and developing ways to explain the good news to them in order to show the gospel's relevance to them. Peter asked Cornelius questions (v 29) so that he could understand where he was coming from.

5. **Which of the elements of the gospel outlined in question 2 do you find hardest to understand and explain to others? Help each other to think about ways in which you might more easily explain this part of the gospel message to others.**

People may struggle both to understand these things and to explain them effectively. You may find as a leader that there are people in your group able to give a fluent explanation—but which is expressed in language that only a believer would understand! Gently help them to see the issue. There are a number of books and other resources listed on page 144 that explain the gospel in engaging, accessible ways.

During this question, which might take up the bulk of your Bible-study time, you should carefully correct wrong views, and encourage people to both understand and practice forms of words and illustrations that will enable them to feel more confident about making and taking opportunities to share the gospel.

OPTIONAL: Split the group into pairs and get them to practice explaining the gospel to each other, using words that anyone might understand.

6. Cornelius may have thought he didn't "qualify" to receive the gospel. Are there people like that today?

Notice that Peter says to Cornelius and his friends: "You yourselves know what happened" (v 37). It seems that Cornelius' problem was not that he did not know the facts of the gospel, but either that he did not understand their significance or, more likely, that he did not realize that the gospel was for him, a Gentile. It needed Peter to affirm what he had himself had only recently understood: that God does not show partiality (v 34) and that EVERYONE who believes in Christ is forgiven (v 43), including Gentiles (see question 7).

Many of us instinctively think that some people who have committed heinous crimes are not worthy of the gospel. We tend to assume that there are whole categories of people who have no interest or are "enemies" in some way—those from other religious groups, etc.

But there are also many outwardly "good" people who consistently fail to understand that the gospel is for them. Maybe there are some even within your congregation. Perhaps they have bought into a gospel of good works. They may appear outwardly to be very religious and (as with Cornelius) more spiritual and devoted than many Christians, but they have never quite seen that forgiveness as a gift of grace is for them.

7. How did Peter show Cornelius that the gospel invitation was for Gentiles such as him (v 34, 43)?

Peter was not afraid to share his own growing understanding of God's revelation on this subject. He says: *"Truly I understand that God shows no partiality"* and he sees that God's revelation of this truth has been visible in the Old Testament all the time: *"All the prophets bear witness that everyone who believes..."* He underlines the truth that the gospel is for anyone with a pulse—whatever their background, history or condition.

8. What can we learn from this for our own evangelism?

- We may need to emphasize some parts of the message to fit the particular needs and life situations of some people. Eg: emphasizing God's compassionate love to those who are needy or unloved; or underlining God's judgment to those who are confident of their own self-righteousness.

- We can be humble and honest about our own lack of understanding, or our growing understanding, of the things of God.
- We must listen and work out where someone is coming from, and what issues they struggle to understand.

FOR YOURSELF: What do I need to work harder at in my understanding of the gospel, and in my skills at articulating it? Are there ways in which I can be of help to, or seek help from, others in the group?

Make a note of the things individuals are struggling to understand or explain. If there is a pattern here, it might be that something could be organized church-wide to redress the problem. Otherwise, if you are able to, it would be good to work out how you could continue to help each other hone these skills as you meet together.

It can be useful to meet one on one to talk about these things, but there is really no substitute for actually doing it. Role play can be helpful, but putting people in a situation where they can speak with someone who is not a Christian is even better training. Does your church have an active door-to-door visitation program? Might there be an opportunity for some street evangelism in your area?

FOR YOUR CHURCH: How might we unconsciously give the impression in how we "do" church that some people don't "qualify" for the gospel? What steps can we take to make clear that the gospel invitation is for everyone?

Of course, the answer to this question will depend on your context.

Pray

FOR YOURSELF: Pray for an opportunity this week to talk about at least one part of the gospel with one of the people you are praying for.

FOR YOUR WHOLE CHURCH: Pray that you would grow in knowledge of the gospel, which will enable you all to speak clearly and helpfully to others.

FURTHER READING

I have found that when I present the simple message of the gospel of Jesus Christ, with authority, quoting from the very Word of God—he takes that message and drives it supernaturally into the human heart.
Billy Graham

Our business is to present the Christian faith in modern terms, not to propagate modern thought clothed in Christian terms. Confusion here is fatal.
J.I. Packer

Books

- *Honest Evangelism, especially chapter 5 (Rico Tice)*
- *Know and Tell the Gospel (John Chapman)*
- *The Gospel and Personal Evangelism, especially chapters 2 and 5 (Mark Dever)*
- *Speaking of Jesus (Mack Stiles)*
- *Tell the Truth (Will Metzger)*

Apologetics:
- *The Reason for God: Belief in an Age of Skepticism (Tim Keller)*
- *If You Could Ask God One Question (Paul Williams & Barry Cooper)*

Gospel Outlines:
- *Two Ways To Live: The Choice We All Face (Tony Payne and Phillip Jensen)*
- *Bridge To Life (The Navigators)*
- *Jesus: Who, Why, So What? (Christianity Explored Ministries)*
- *The Story (Spread Truth Ministries)*

Online

- *christianityexplored.org*
- *Don't Just Share your Testimony: gospelshapedchurch.org/resources271*

LEADER'S REFLECTIONS

SESSION 8:

HOW DO WE SPEAK?

EFFECTIVE EVANGELISM IS USUALLY PART OF A
CONVERSATION, AND HAPPENS IN THE CONTEXT OF
AN EXISTING FRIENDSHIP. OUR GOSPEL
PROCLAMATION NEEDS TO MAKE SENSE TO PEOPLE,
AND TO CONNECT TO THEIR LIVES, HOPES AND FEARS.
WE MAY HAVE THE GREATEST GOSPEL EXPLANATION
MEMORIZED IN OUR HEADS, BUT IF WE NEVER WORK
OUT HOW TO INTRODUCE IT INTO OUR INTERACTIONS
AND FRIENDSHIPS, IT WILL STAY IN OUR HEADS!
SO IN THIS SESSION, WE CONSIDER HOW WE SPEAK
THE GOSPEL INTO REAL PEOPLE'S REAL LIVES.

TALK OUTLINE

8.1 ● Our game plan for evangelism has this objective: to communicate the gospel faithfully to those God has put around us. How can we do this well?

● **WE CAN SPEAK TO PEOPLE KNOWLEDGEABLY**
- We cannot assume that people have any biblical knowledge or worldview.
- Concepts like "sin," "the curse," "Jesus Christ," "faith," and "salvation" are essential to the gospel, but often misunderstood by non-believers. We need to be able to explain them in a way that people can understand. Can we?

8.2 ● **WE CAN SPEAK TO PEOPLE INTENTIONALLY**
- "Attractional" ministries no longer draw people to church; but God uses (as he always has) an attractive message through the words of an attractive people.
- We don't need to do more; we need to do what we do differently. We can reorient our daily, weekly and monthly activities around evangelism by having:
  - a **community component** (involving another member of our church);
  - a **missional component** (by involving a non-Christian);
  - a **gospel component** (by identifying opportunities to talk about Jesus).

8.3 ● **WE CAN SPEAK TO PEOPLE ATTENTIVELY**
- We live in a distracted culture; but it's important for us to *listen* to people.
- We listen for people making comments about life that are really about creation, fall, redemption or restoration (for more on this, see pages 153-156).

● **WE CAN SPEAK TO PEOPLE THOUGHTFULLY**
When we listen to others, we hear how their hearts cry for salvation. We must compassionately show how the gospel answers pain and brokenness.

● **WE CAN SPEAK TO PEOPLE PATIENTLY**
Sometimes we share the gospel and nothing seems to happen. Be a patient and faithful friend; it is God who brings the growth, in his timing.

You can download a full transcript of these talks at
WWW.GOSPELSHAPEDCHURCH.ORG/OUTREACH/TALKS

 HOW DO WE SPEAK?

* *Ask the group members to turn to Session 8 on page 125 of the Handbook.*

Discuss

Last week we looked at the key elements of the gospel message. As you have thought about these during the week, has anything struck you?

> People may have been struck afresh by the truth of one of the key elements, noticing how one particular element is especially relevant for a non-Christian they know, or maybe realizing they didn't understand the gospel message as clearly as they had thought. This is an opportunity for the group to be encouraged by what they've been learning, and also, if necessary, for you to clarify any points people are unsure of. But there is no need to spend time discussing this if the group have not been particularly struck by anything during the week.

▶ **WATCH DVD 8.1** (5 min 5 sec) **OR LISTEN TO TALK 8.1** (see page 148)

* *Encourage the group to make notes as they watch the DVD or listen to the talk. There is space for notes on page 127 of the Handbook.*

Discuss

Sin, Jesus Christ, faith, salvation.

Choose one of these words or names that were mentioned in the talk. Discuss how you might explain it simply to someone with very little knowledge of how it is used in the Bible. Do this without using the word itself (eg: explain what faith is without using the word "faith").

> All of these terms are used in the secular world, even "Jesus Christ" (though mainly as a swear word)—but a non-Christian's understanding of each of these words may be very different from the biblical use. That's why it's important not to use

the word itself when explaining what it means. (Note: If explaining "Jesus Christ," suggest to the group that they can use the word "Jesus," but not use his title, "Christ.")

It's tempting to try and create a "perfect" definition of each word, but this may not be helpful. It's more important that people come up with a form of words that they find easy to remember and explain, and that does not assume any knowledge in a hearer. Having said that, the following summaries may be helpful.

Sin: can be described as "missing the mark" (eg: in archery or target shooting) or "falling short" of a standard (Romans 3:23). It is an attitude of the heart, rather than a list of "wrong things" we do (Mark 7:21-23). It is rebellion against God's rule, doing what *we* want instead of what *God* wants. It is taking God's gifts without thanking him or even recognizing his existence. We need to make clear the difference between "sins" and "sin." Things we do wrong (sins) reveal the big heart problem (sin) of rebellion against God.

Jesus Christ: is both a name and a title. The name "Jesus" means "God saves" (Matthew 1:21). It tells us who he is: *he is God.* It tells us what he does: *he saves us.* "Christ" is not Jesus' surname—it is his title. It is a Greek word. The same word in Hebrew is "Messiah." They both mean "the anointed one," which can be explained as "God's chosen King." In the Old Testament, a man would be anointed with oil to make them a king (eg: 1 Samuel 16:13); and God promised to send an ultimate "anointed one" to rule and save his people (2 Samuel 7:12-13). Jesus is that King—the One who came to fulfill all God's promises to his people.

Faith: is taking God at his word and trusting that his promises will come true. It is an action, not a feeling, which means that "trust" is a helpful word to use when explaining it. It is a gift from God (Ephesians 2:8), not something we earn, deserve or work toward.

Salvation: means being saved from sin and its consequences, and brought into right relationship with God for eternity. It is to be rescued from a situation that we cannot free ourselves from (ie: facing God's judgment and wrath in hell), and for an experience we could not bring ourselves into (ie: eternal life with God in his perfect, restored world). The way that God offers us salvation is through Jesus' death and resurrection (Acts 4:12).

What illustration or story might you use?

There are many. The best stories are often ones from our own lives or experiences (for instance, a time when we ourselves have been rescued by someone can illustrate salvation). And as we grow in experience in evangelism, we learn to match an illustration or explanation to the person we are speaking to—to their life and interests. Let your group share any they have found particularly helpful in evangelism. Below are some suggestions, but they are only suggestions—there is no right answer here, and you may well choose to use one of your own stories.

Sin: Imagine a pirate on a pirate ship. However hard or lazily he works, however kind or selfish he is toward others, it does not really matter. What matters is that he is working on a pirate ship, in rebellion against the rightful authority. As sinners, this is what we are like. We may be nice people or nasty people, but we are by nature rebels because we refuse to accept God's authority. OR God is perfect, and so the standard for entrance to his presence is perfection. 100% is the pass mark. Imagine your life for the next week is an exam. See if you can think, say and do only what is in obedience to God's commands. If I'm honest, I know I couldn't, no matter how hard I try—because I sin.

Jesus Christ: Who do you think the three greatest leaders of our country have been? What qualities made them so great? What flaws did they have? Imagine a leader who combined all those qualities, who exhibited none of those flaws, and who never grew weary or handed over power. What a country his or hers would be! This is the kind of ruler God promised throughout the Old Testament—an all-powerful, all-just, all-wise, all-loving King, who crucially would never die and so would be able to reign forever. And as Jesus lived on earth, by what he said and did he proved he is that perfect King, and gave a glimpse of what life in eternity under his rule is like.

Faith: We all have faith in things, because faith is absolute trust. You trust your car will get you from one place to another safely. You trust the chair you're sitting on to bear your weight. When the Bible speaks about faith, it means what are we trusting in for our death. Our own ideas (eg: there is no afterlife)? Our own goodness (ie: I'm good enough to get a place in heaven)? Or Jesus Christ, to give us a place in eternity? The Bible says the only person that can bear the weight of our death is Jesus—he is the only one who can be trusted to take us through death and judgment, to eternal life.

Salvation: Imagine a person is drowning in the middle of the ocean, with no hope of swimming to shore. Then a helicopter appears, a rope comes down, a man comes down the rope, attaches the drowning person to that rope, and they are winched up, and flown to shore and safety. From a position of absolutely no hope, they have been rescued. In the death and resurrection of Jesus Christ, God has come to us to rescue us from a position of no hope and certain death, to his presence and to safety.

What alternative words are there that helpfully explain the real meaning of these ideas?

See the explanations for each term on pages 150-152, and the alternative words used there.

▶ **WATCH DVD 8.2** (3 min 17 sec) **OR LISTEN TO TALK 8.2** (see page 148)

* *Encourage the group to make notes as they watch the DVD or listen to the talk. There is space for notes on page 128 of the Handbook.*

Discuss

List three things you already do regularly that you might invite people to do with you.

If people are struggling to think of anything, why not suggest they flick through their calendar to see what's coming up in the next two weeks? Encourage them to include things they do at home, at work or in the neighborhood.

What gospel opportunities might there already be in these activities that you have never thought about before?

Encourage the group to help one another come up with creative ideas. You may want to have an example of your own ready so that you can start the discussion if necessary.

▶ **WATCH DVD 8.3** (4 min 23 sec) **OR LISTEN TO TALK 8.3** (see page 148)

* *Encourage the group to make notes as they watch the DVD or listen to the talk.*
There is space for notes on page 129 of the Handbook.

In the DVD, Erik talks about the timeline of salvation. If we listen attentively to people, we can hear them talking about these four things:

CREATION | FALL | REDEMPTION | RESTORATION

Think about the following sentences. Can you see ways in which they link with one or more elements of the timeline above? How might you move from each one to an aspect of the gospel message?

In the list below we have given some possible links. It's not necessary for your group to come up with all of these, or even agree with them all! The aim is to get some practice in seeing how relatively common topics of conversation can be linked to the timeline of salvation.

Further, it can be intimidating to someone who has never thought about these categories before to be asked to work out during a conversation which category someone is speaking about, and at the same time to see how to turn the conversation to an aspect of the Bible's worldview. So encourage your group to think at the end of each day in the coming week about interactions they have had, and try to work out which of the four categories people's comments fit into. They might also consider how they could continue a conversation with that person, picking up on a comment they made and connecting to the gospel from it. For instance: "I was thinking overnight about what you'd said about young people's lack of respect. Where do you think that lack of respect comes from? I wonder if you ever see it in your own life, too? I know I do in mine!"

"I saw our new grandson for the first time and was amazed at how cute he is. You should see his tiny, perfect fingers and toes, and his lovely smile."

Creation: We might say something like: "It's not surprising he's so beautiful—when God created our world he said that everything was good, so we'd still expect to see that" (Genesis 1:31).

"When I think of young people today, I despair. They show no respect."

Fall: "I think young people have always been rebels; they just don't bother hiding it anymore. The Bible says all people rebel against God. They choose to run lives their way rather than his way."

"We're saving hard for a rainy day, but you never know how the stock market will go."

Redemption: "There does seem to be great security in having a bit more money, doesn't there? I know I often think that way. Is there anything you'll need that you think money can't buy?"

Fall: "Ah, that's always the problem with shares, isn't it? You can never know for sure that they'll come through for you when you need them. I guess most things in this life are uncertain. It's why I love knowing that God will never let me down, and will do for me the things that money simply cannot."

"I'm really pleased/worried that _____ won the election. They are just what this country needs / going to make things even worse."

Fall: "Things do seem to be unraveling a bit, don't they? Do you think we put too much hope in politics to solve all our problems?"

Redemption: "What are you hoping they'll do for the country? Is there a danger we'll ask too much of them—are there limits to what a politician can do? Why do you think we put so much hope in our politicians, and get so disappointed or angry when they don't deliver?"

Restoration: "What are the things a politician can't achieve, and what are the things they can't take away? Do you ever wish the future was so secure that it couldn't be messed up by politicians?!"

"We're looking forward to retirement next year. We have a special trip planned to celebrate."

Restoration: "What is it about retirement that you're looking forward to? Do you have a plan for what you'll do after your retirement? To be honest, I think less about my retirement than my eternity, because I know the second will last a lot longer than the first!"

"They've just made more lay-offs at work. I'm worried I might be next."

Fall: "I'm so sorry to hear that. I'll certainly pray for you. I guess the upside might be that it reminds you that there's more to life than work. Which is great, isn't it? Because work is frustrating when we have it, and worrying when we might lose it. Why do you think work never quite satisfies us, or gives us proper security?"

"Family is the most important thing, of course. That's why we're here—to bring up the next generation and see them happy and settled."

Creation: "Why do you think we have this inbuilt commitment to family? I wonder if you've ever thought of God as being a family himself—a trinity of Father, Son and Spirit—and that that's where we get our desire and love for family from?

Redemption: "Sounds like you're putting a lot of pressure on your family to deliver all you hope they will! If they're the most important thing, would that make life not worth living if they weren't around, or let you down?"

Restoration: "If the primary purpose of each generation is to raise the next one, then it strikes me that we don't have much purpose at all; we just raise kids, so they raise kids, and they raise kids, forever, and we're long forgotten. Do you think there might be more to life and the future than that?"

"We are moving next week. After a difficult few years it will be good to have a fresh start."

Redemption: "What are you trying to escape? Is there anything you're worried that the move won't fix?"

Restoration: "Where are you moving to? What is it that you think will be better there than here? Do you ever worry that you might be demanding too much of this move—to deliver perfection? I wonder if you're expecting this new place to be heaven. I have to say that when I consider our future, it's a great relief to know that while I will probably never solve all my issues and regrets in this life, one day I'll "move" to a perfect place with a proper fresh start."

"I'm spending every evening at night school. It's the only way to get ahead."

Redemption: "What hopes are you pinning on getting more of an education? What problems or weaknesses are you hoping it will solve? Are you hoping that getting a better job and higher salary will deliver you the life you want, or would there need to be more to it than that?"

Pray

 1 CORINTHIANS 3:6-7

⁶ I [Paul] planted, Apollos watered, but God gave the growth. ⁷ So neither he who plants nor he who waters is anything, but only God who gives the growth.

"Our responsibility as disciples of Christ is to plant and water the seeds of the gospel; it is God who causes the growth." Ask God to help you to be ready to take gospel opportunities when they arise, but also to be patient as you wait for the Holy Spirit to do his work in an unbeliever's life.

Ask God to help you explain important gospel concepts in a way that is clear, simple and easy for a non-Christian to relate to.

Pray for an opportunity to invite a neighbor or friend to join you in one of your regular activities.

DAILY BIBLE DEVOTIONALS

These personal studies walk through 1 Peter 3:14-18, focusing on the context for our witnessing in a world that rejects Christ; and the heart, words and manner of the gospel witness.

SERMONS

OPTION ONE: 1 CORINTHIANS 3:5-8

This is one of the passages that Erik bases his DVD presentation on, which could be expanded upon in a sermon.

OPTION TWO: JOHN 4:1-42

This is the passage the Bible study is based on (see next page), which could also be expanded upon in a sermon.

OPTION THREE: 1 THESSALONIANS 2:2-12

This passage is not mentioned in this material, but picks up on several of the themes of this session. As Paul recounts his mission trip to Thessalonica, we see from his example that the gospel must be declared:
- Faithfully, even when it is hard (v 2).
- Honestly, which pleases God (v 3-6).
- Lovingly, through our lives as well as our words (v 7-12).

If one of your Sunday sermons is to be based on the theme of this session, church members will find a page to write notes on the sermon on page 139 of their Handbooks.

🔍 BIBLE STUDY

AIM: The main teaching session this week opened up questions about how we talk with others about the gospel—in particular, how we can live in ways that grow our opportunities for reaching out to others. This Bible study looks at the way the Lord Jesus modeled that kind of evangelism, and provokes our thinking about specific ways we can live as "people on mission."

NOTE: Unlike in the other Bible studies, in this study the apply questions appear throughout the study, rather than being left till the end.

Discuss

Who do you go to when you have a difficult question about something at work or in your personal life? Why do you choose them, rather than someone else?

> This is to get people talking about who we talk with and why. It opens up our consideration of the kind of character we want to cultivate in order to be more effective witnesses for Christ.

> **Alternative Discussion Question:** Have you had a bad experience of calling a "customer care" helpline? What did they do that was poor? What did you end up thinking about the company you were calling or the product you were asking for help with?

 READ JOHN 4:1-30

Samaritans were considered a heretical sect by the Jews, and were therefore hated and regarded as racially impure. In Jesus' time, women were also regarded as second-class citizens.

1. What does Jesus do in this passage that makes him "approachable" and opens up the conversation with the woman?

- He asks for help (v 7).

- He initiates a conversation (v 7, 10).
- He shows no partiality or judgmentalism regarding her religion, sex, nationality or social status.

2. How can we be similarly approachable as people?

- By being friendly. Many Christians give off an air of "we've got it all together" or "we've got the answers" in a way that can seem very superior in attitude to others. Show a genuine interest in people and spend time with them.
- By asking for help. Sometimes we feel we need to appear to be "the people who have got it together" and who are self-sufficient. When we ask others for advice or help—with advice, children, practical problems—it makes it clear that we want to develop a genuine relationship and friendship.
- By being proactive in general discussions about life, community issues, etc. as well as in spiritual things.
- By not being judgmental with people. Jesus is for everyone with a pulse.

People can easily see us as "preachers" who are disinterested in others as people. Or else as so "holy" that we do not seem to be approachable when they have genuine questions. On the other hand, we can be so "approachable" and "warm" that we fail to give a clear and faithful message when we are asked. Question 3 opens up this issue.

How approachable are you as a church?

Discuss whether your church (probably unconsciously) looks as though or sounds as though it is for a particular "type" of person, or not for those of a particular background. Would it be the kind of place where people felt free to ask questions, and would not be made to look stupid? Is it somewhere that people feel welcomed sincerely? In what ways might your church appear more judgmental than loving?

3. How does Jesus use statements and language to move the conversation toward discussing gospel truth (v 13-14, 16, 26)? Can you expand on this from the way in which Jesus deals with people in other incidents from the Gospels?

- He makes intriguing statements—which hint at the truth without stating it, which provoke the hearer into asking further questions. He then goes on to explain the truth to them.

- He is not afraid of making a plain statement of truth (v 26).
- He uses vivid word pictures (v 14).
- He illustrates from everyday life (v 13).
- He uses plain language.
- He uses questions and statements to reveal and diagnose people's needs (v 16—see also Jesus' encounter with the rich young ruler in Mark 10:18; or Peter in Mark 8:29; or Simon the Pharisee in Luke 7:41-42).
- He tells stories (parables) extensively.

4. What can we learn from Jesus' example for our own evangelism?

Get the group to think of how each of Jesus' "methods" above would look in their own lives and conversations. Notice how "earthy" Jesus was—because he was speaking to a woman at a well, he began to explain the offer of the gospel in terms of water. As your group talk, watch out for stories and ways of saying things that reflect a bygone culture. Eg: stories from history that might be irrelevant for most modern listeners. We have an internal Christian culture that can warp our perception of what really communicates well with outsiders!

How can we keep the way we express the gospel "fresh"?

- Keep thinking about contemporary illustrations and stories that make good connections with the gospel.
- Read modern books and magazines so that we will understand the mode of expression and contact points with those we are trying to reach.
- Read new evangelistic books regularly, to get fresh ideas on how to explain and illustrate the gospel message.
- Encourage each other, and your preachers, to work at expressing things clearly and simply.

5. What elements of the gospel message that we have seen from previous weeks does Jesus go on to explain to the woman?

- He speaks about the gift of eternal life (v 14).
- He speaks about God as personal and relational ("Father" v 23).
- He helps her see that she is looking in the wrong place for meaning and fulfillment (v 16).

- He reveals himself as the truth-telling Messiah promised by the Old Testament (v 25).

What does he not say?

Several elements of the gospel message are not mentioned at all (eg: his death and resurrection, and her need to repent). Jesus doesn't say everything!

Additional question: When might it be OK just to say part of the gospel? When is the right moment to say everything?

Help the group to see that sometimes it is good to say just one thing well as the opportunity arises, but the direction and focus should always be toward Jesus (*"I who speak to you am he,"* v 26). When we are able, and if they are willing to hear, we could explain the whole of the gospel message.

6. **How does Jesus deal with the woman raising a controversial topic, possibly to take the conversation in a different direction, in verse 20? What is the lesson for us?**

   - He does not ignore it, but answers it carefully.
   - He answers it in a way that leads to the gospel.

When people ask questions, we need to respond properly to them. They may be of ultimate concern to them even if they seem unimportant or irrelevant to us; they may be blocking their progress in considering the claims of Christ on their lives. But we mustn't think that answering a question is enough in itself. In fact, you can only understand the answer to many questions, particularly about sin and suffering, if you see the answer within the context of the whole Bible message.

You could point out that one useful way to reply to a question would be to say: "That's a really important question, which Jesus gives a compelling answer to. But to understand how Christians think about this, you need to see the big picture of what God is doing in the world—would you mind if I took a minute or two to explain that to you?"

7. The conversation ends abruptly when the disciples return (v 27)—and Jesus allows the woman to walk off (v 28)! How would you feel about a fruitful conversation ending like that? What happens subsequently?

- We might be frustrated that a conversation finishes without us being able to "close the deal" or say everything we wanted to. But this is the nature of conversations! We do not always get the chance or time to say all we would like to, in exactly the way we would like to. But we must say what we are able to, and then pray that God would use what we did say, rather than panicking about what we did not have opportunity to say.
- In this case, the woman's intrigue causes her enthusiastically to invite and bring other people to Jesus (v 28-30). Jesus' initial conversation with the woman is not the only gospel opportunity he has with her and the other people in her town; he has the chance to share "his word" with the town for two days (v 40).

Make the point that most people's "journey to faith" takes several years, and involves perhaps hundreds of conversations and encounters with Christians—sermons, books, events, casual conversations, Bible studies, etc. We can rejoice to be faithfully a small part of that, and leave the result to God. *"I planted, Apollos watered, but God gave the growth"* (1 Corinthians 3:6).

8. Jesus' conversation with the woman started as she went about her normal daily routine, and as Jesus asked her for something very ordinary: a drink. What kinds of things do people talk about in general? How might these become an opportunity for talking about God and the gospel?

People talk about all kinds of things—the weather, their holidays, illness in their family, parenting difficulties, problems at work, things they have seen on TV or read in books, and political and social questions of the day.

People respond well to a more "testimonial" expression of the gospel, as opposed to what they perceive as preaching. Get the group to contribute from their own experience.

Pray

FOR YOUR GROUP: Pray that you would encourage each other to be more open to outsiders. What could you do that might involve more outsiders being involved?

FOR YOUR CHURCH: Ask God to bring seekers to you; and ask God to make you seekers of others.

FURTHER READING

Being an extrovert isn't essential to evangelism—obedience and love are.
Rebecca Manley Pippert

Cruel wretches are we to our friends, that will rather suffer them to go quietly to hell, than we will anger them, or hazard our reputation with them.
Richard Baxter

Books

- *The Gospel and Personal Evangelism*, chapter 4 (Mark Dever)
- *Tactics* (Greg Koukl)
- *Out of the Saltshaker & into the World* (Rebecca Manley Pippert)
- *Speaking of Jesus* (Mack Stiles)
- *The Unchurched Next Door* (Thom Rainer)
- *The Unbelievable Gospel* (Jonathan Dodson)
- *Questioning Evangelism* (Randy Newman)
- *Becoming a Contagious Christian* (Bill Hybels & Mark Mittelberg)

Online

- *How Your Church can Grow in Evangelism* (video) gospelshapedchurch.org/resources281
- *A Simple and Radical Key to Evangelistic Breakthrough* gospelshapedchurch.org/resources282

LEADER'S REFLECTIONS

SESSION 9:

HOW DO WE KEEP GOING?

GOSPEL WITNESS IS A LIFELONG COMMAND TO US,
AND SO IT REQUIRES A LIFELONG COMMITMENT
FROM US. ALL TOO OFTEN, A PERSON'S OR CHURCH'S
EVANGELISM RISES WITH A TEACHING SERIES OR
MISSIONAL SEASON, AND THEN FALLS AGAIN WHEN
THE FOCUS SHIFTS ELSEWHERE.
SO, AS WE COME TO THE LAST SESSION IN THIS
CURRICULUM, WE NEED TO CONSIDER HOW WE CAN
HELP OURSELVES AND ENCOURAGE EACH OTHER TO
KEEP GOING IN OUR EVANGELISM.

TALK OUTLINE

9.1 • How do we make sure we keep obeying Christ's command to make disciples?

• **BE CONVINCED THAT THE GOSPEL IS OF FIRST IMPORTANCE**
1 Corinthians 15:3: It's the most important thing a church can be concerned with.

• **CALIBRATE ALL OF LIFE AND MINISTRY BY THE GOSPEL**
Ministries can quickly lose focus; but each one must be shaped by the gospel.

• **BE LEADERS WHO MODEL MAKING AND TRAINING DISCIPLES**
Teachers must model evangelism; members must pray for and encourage them.

• **HELP PEOPLE THINK OF THEIR LIVES AS A STEWARDSHIP**
Our life is a stewardship; we serve others with the gospel and give glory to God.

9.2 • **REMIND PEOPLE THEIR CHURCH IS A MISSIONARY WORK**
Otherwise, an outreach culture will not flourish. Every church was once a plant.

• **PRIORITIZE EVANGELISM IN THE CHURCH BUDGET**
The gospel should be of "first importance" in church meetings and budgets.

• **BE TRAINED TO MAKE AND TRAIN DISCIPLES** *Ephesians 4:11-15*
God intends for us to grow. What area of outreach do you need more help with?

• **KEEP PRAYING FOR AND CELEBRATING CONVERSIONS**
Heaven rejoices when a sinner repents (Luke 15:10), and so can, and must, we!

• **PLANT CHURCHES** *Matthew 28:19-20*
Church planting is a consequence of the Great Commission; more disciples need more churches!

• **CONCLUSION:** "Evangelism? Yes—that's my job!"

You can download a full transcript of these talks at
WWW.GOSPELSHAPEDCHURCH.ORG/OUTREACH/TALKS

HOW DO WE KEEP GOING?

* *Ask the group members to turn to Session 9 on page 141 of the Handbook.*

Discuss

Have you ever taken part in a sporting activity, big school project, weight-loss program or home-improvement project that has taken a long time? Did you ever feel you wanted to give up? How did you keep yourself going?

This question is designed to start the group thinking about projects they've been involved in where they were motivated to succeed but still found it hard to persevere. Hopefully, everyone who has done this course is feeling motivated to share the gospel. Today's session will look at some of the ways in which we can help each other to keep going, even when things are tough or discouraging, and not let the excitement we feel at the moment dry up.

▶ **WATCH DVD 9.1** (7 min 26 sec) **OR LISTEN TO TALK 9.1** (see page 168)

* *Encourage the group to make notes as they watch the DVD or listen to the talk. There is space for notes on page 143 of the Handbook.*

"Ministry involves different types of people with different types of gifts— all working together to advance the gospel. God gives us the privilege of serving him in this way."

How does the example of others inspire you to be more proactive in evangelism? How can you, in turn, inspire others by your example?

Possible answers might include: that it's inspiring to hear about someone sharing the gospel for the first time; it's encouraging when someone who is shy makes an opportunity to talk about Jesus (and it encourages the rest of us that we can do this too); we may be inspired when we hear about a particular event (eg:

GOSPEL SHAPED OUTREACH

if someone hosts a barbecue for their neighbors, we may realize we could do something similar).

How can we encourage our leaders to lead us in evangelism?

It's easy to think that leaders find evangelism easier than the rest of us! But we need to pray for them too (Matthew 9:38) and let them know we are praying. Perhaps a home group could commit to praying for a leader and their personal evangelism, asking regularly for specific people and events to pray for. Ask if you can give practical support such as babysitting so that a leader and his wife can spend an evening with a non-Christian couple.

This course has focused on the need for both individual evangelism by believers, and for the church as a whole to be a missionary family. Pray that your minister/elders will lead the church in a way that is faithful to the gospel and attractive to non-Christians.

NOTE: If your group have specific suggestions for how they would like to be encouraged or equipped in evangelism by their church leadership, tell your group that you will pass those ideas on to the leaders.

We often think about stewardship in terms of the money and possessions we own, and the gifts and time we have been given. Think of some possessions and gifts you have. How could you use them for evangelism? How could selfishness prevent you from doing this?

Try to encourage a mix of answers here and especially, not just to focus on "big" possessions such as a house or car. All of us, no matter how rich or poor, have gifts from God we can share. Examples could include:

- *Skills:* If someone is good at car maintenance, sewing, decorating, etc., how could they use these to build relationships with those around them? (A selfish response might be to want to keep these skills just to make our own car, clothes, house a bit better rather than helping others.)
- *Time:* A retired person, or someone who isn't working, may be able to offer time to give practical help, visit someone who is ill and do their shopping, or just be available to talk to someone who is lonely. (A selfish response might be to spend all our extra time on the sofa watching movies.)

170

- *Car:* Could we do a car-share for commuting to work? (If we are selfish, we like to enjoy the travel time by ourselves.)
- *Money:* The issue here isn't how much we have, but how we use it. If the gospel if "of first importance" (1 Corinthians 15:3), how much of our money are we giving to it? (It's tempting to see our money, especially if we work hard for it, as all our own. But it is a gift from God, designed for sharing—like a large box of chocolates!)

We don't own the gospel: we are stewards of it. How will this impact the way we think about our evangelism as individuals and as a church?

- It is a gift to give away, not to keep to ourselves—so we must share it whenever we can.
- Sharing it should not be a burden, but a joy.
- *"God has given us life, health, relationships, influence, jobs, neighborhoods, all for the purpose of being faithful, and giving him the glory. One major aspect of this is to see our responsibility to share the gospel with others."*
- *"A church that is made by the gospel must also be shaped by the gospel."* Your church only exists because of the gospel, and so it has a responsibility to share the good news faithfully in the surrounding area.

▶ **WATCH DVD 9.2** (7 min 19 sec) **OR LISTEN TO TALK 9.2** (see page 168)

- *Encourage the group to make notes as they watch the DVD or listen to the talk. There is space for notes on page 145 of the Handbook.*

What further help do you think you need to grow in confidence and skill in sharing the gospel with others?

Ask the group if there's anything they particularly feel they are lacking. But also have some suggestions ready of resources that can help and of support you can offer. For example, helpful books or DVDs; further training; meeting to hone their testimonies, etc. There is a list of helpful resources on page 180.

Areas in which you may want to offer help or training include:
- one-on-one Bible study
- answering tricky questions from the Bible (simple apologetics)
- help to think through how to explain Biblical concepts and words clearly

• help to know which Bible passages will speak into areas where people are thinking, struggling or confused.

Over these nine sessions, how have you been excited about evangelism?

Encourage honest answers to this and the following three questions. Listen out for any comments that show that someone may need more help or encouragement in a particular area, and also anything that suggests it may be helpful to make some tweaks to this course material before running it again.

How have you been challenged?

How have you been equipped?

How have you been changed?

 MATTHEW 28:18-20

> [18] *And Jesus came and said to them, "All authority in heaven and on earth has been given to me.* [19] *Go therefore and make disciples of all nations, baptizing them in the name of the Father and of the Son and of the Holy Spirit,* [20] *teaching them to observe all that I have commanded you. And behold, I am with you always, to the end of the age."*

What encouragements and/or discouragements have you had in your own outreach while doing this course?

This is an opportunity to hear again how group members have been getting on with sharing the gospel message with others. Do include an update from each person on the two people they've been wanting to share the gospel with, but don't limit yourselves to that. You have been praying since Session 1 that God will help you to make and take evangelistic opportunities, so it's likely that he has done this more widely than just the two people you have each focused on.

For those who are feeling discouraged, encourage them (and the group) to think of a scriptural truth you've seen in the course which can counter that particular discouragement (eg: if someone has shared the gospel but feels they did not do so very well, it is great to remember that God is the one who changes hearts, and he can use the most stuttering gospel explanation).

Some will be encouraged—rejoice with them, and give the glory to God. Some may be discouraged—listen to and pray with them, and promise to keep praying in the coming weeks.

Pray

"A church that is made by the gospel must also be shaped by the gospel." Pray that this would be true of your church.

Tell the group the names of two people you want to share the gospel with this month. These may be the same people you have already been praying for, or this could be an opportunity to add two more. Pray for each of these people by name, that the Lord will give you opportunities to tell them the good news about Jesus.

DAILY BIBLE DEVOTIONALS

The last set of devotionals focuses on a passage that has been mentioned in several sections: Matthew 9:35 –10:8. Here, we see Jesus' compassion for the lost; his prayer for workers; his call to his people to go and proclaim his kingdom; and his training for the mission field.

SERMONS

OPTION ONE: LUKE 15:1-10

This is one of the passages that Erik mentions in his DVD talk, and which could be used in a sermon, enjoying the truth that God is a missionary God, who rejoices when the lost are found.

OPTION TWO: 2 CORINTHIANS 5:11-20

This is the passage the Bible study is based on (see next page), which could also be expanded upon in a sermon.

OPTION THREE: 2 CORINTHIANS 4:1-18

This passage is not mentioned in this material, but picks up on several of the themes of this session. We do not lose heart in evangelism because:
- God works in unbelievers' hearts as we proclaim Christ (v 1-6).
- God shows his life-giving power through weak people (v 7-15).
- God will bring us through hardships to eternal glory (v 16-18).

If one of your Sunday sermons is to be based on the theme of this session, church members will find a page to write notes on the sermon on page 155 of their Handbooks.

BIBLE STUDY

AIM: In the main talk this week, we looked at how we can ensure that evangelism remains at the heart of our church life. In this final Bible-study session, we'll try to tie together everything we have been thinking about by looking at the motivation for evangelism, and what a privilege it is to be part of God's mission in the world.

Discuss

If you could be an ambassador of any country (except your own), in any country in the world, what would you choose, and why?

Just a bit of fun to get people thinking about what is involved in representing someone else in important matters.

 READ 2 CORINTHIANS 5:11-20

* *Get the group to speed read from 4:1 to get the context if you have time.*

1. **Paul has been talking about the work of bringing the gospel to the world. Look back at 4:1, 16; 5:6. What problem is he very aware of? How can this affect us also?**

   ● It is easy to lose heart.
   ● Our courage can fail in evangelism because it is hard and we suffer for it.
   ● So growing discouraged and giving up witnessing is a constant temptation.

2. **What reason does Paul give in verse 11 for keeping going in outreach? What does that mean?**

   ● Knowing the fear of the Lord. It means that we respect and love God more than we fear men.
   ● We care more about God's reputation than our own.
   ● He has commanded us to preach the gospel—so we do so because we fear him.

3. **What reason does Paul give in verse 14 for keeping going in outreach? What effect does that have on him (see v 15-16)?**

- He is controlled (motivated) by the amazing love of Jesus Christ for the world.
- The evidence for the size and scope of his love is his death on the cross (v 15)
- Jesus died for all—so that all could be offered salvation through the cross. So Paul must continue to preach the gospel to all.
- Since Jesus saved me, my life is not my own, but belongs to him. I am called to not live a selfish life anymore, but to live for Jesus, who died and rose again for me (v 15).

What change does it lead to in Paul's view of other people (v16)?

We tend to categorize people in human terms, but because the love, death and resurrection of Christ is the central event of human history, we now look at, and regard all people according to what it teaches us. We now look at people as:

- spiritual beings
- loved by God because Christ died for all
- sinners in need of a Savior
- rebels, who need reconciling to God

4. **What amazing privilege does Paul say we have been given (v 18)? What effect does this have on Paul?**

- We have been entrusted with the ministry of reconciliation—that is, the reconciliation of sinful men and women to a holy God through the finished work of Christ.
- Reconciliation is the will of the Father (v 20).
- Reconciliation is the work of the Son (v 19).
- We are entrusted with a job in this work—to deliver the message.
- Paul does it, and keeps going at it, even when he is facing suffering (6:4).

5. **Paul calls himself an ambassador for Christ (v 20). How is this a helpful picture for us—how does it encourage and protect us?**

- Ambassadors deliver a message on behalf of someone else. They are representatives of another government.
- We are not responsible for making up the message, just delivering it.

- We can be confident that God will not abandon us as his representatives.
- We can speak with authority the message we have been given to deliver.

6. What is the result of gospel preaching (v 17, 19, 20)? How should this motivate us?

- People are made completely new in Jesus.
- Their sins are not counted against them.
- They are reconciled to God.

It is a fantastic and undeserved privilege to be part of the way God brings new life to people. We are part of the way in which God saves people from death and hell to life and eternity. There is no greater joy.

7. Paul uses emotive words to describe the way he goes about sharing the good news with others: persuade (v 11); implore (v 20); appeal (6:1). How will this help us as we tell others?

He wants to persuade others that the gospel is true. He recognizes that the gospel message about Jesus involves both evidence to present, and an argument to be won, about who is in ultimate control of our lives. He knows that Jesus Christ is Lord, and fears him as the Lord of all creation. He wants to persuade others of the identity of Christ, so they in turn will fear him.

But this is not just a salesman's persuasion. We should also be emotionally connected with the outcome. We are speaking to people we love who are lost without Christ. There is a place for imploring and appealing to them to respond. Sometimes people will be convinced by an argument, but also need a direct personal challenge to respond.

How can we sustain a passion for sharing the good news with others over time?

- Keep reminding ourselves of the truths of the gospel.
- Keep rejoicing over our own conversion and salvation.
- Keep rejoicing over the salvation of others.
- Keep reminding ourselves of the desperate plight of those who are lost without Christ.

- Keep remembering that God works through the proclamation of his word by his people—to save people.
- Pray that God would fill us with gratitude for what he has done for us in Christ.

Apply

FOR YOURSELF: Which of the motivations Paul has talked about do I find personally most helpful as I think about being a good steward of the gospel message I have been entrusted with? In what practical ways can I live out this motivation?

Allow the group to "pick a favorite," and talk about why it motivates them. This should be helpful to the rest of the group as they think about the fear of the Lord; the love of Christ; the privilege of being partners in God's mission; and the honor of being an ambassador.

FOR YOUR CHURCH: How can you encourage the leaders of your church to keep evangelism as a central focus in their own lives, and for your church?

Pray

FOR YOURSELF: Pray again for the two friends you have been thinking about over the course, or the two additional people you shared about for prayer in the main session.

FOR YOUR CHURCH: Now that we have reached the end of this course, pray that it would be the start of something, not the end of something.

FURTHER READING

"If there be any one point in which the Christian church ought to keep its fervor at a white heat, it is ... the matter of sending the gospel to a dying world.
C.H. Spurgeon

We should never stop at having won a soul for Christ. By this, we have done only half the work. Every soul won for Christ must be made to be a soul-winner.
Richard Wurmbrand

Books

- *The Gospel and Personal Evangelism, chapter 6 (Mark Dever)*
- *Evangelism: How the Whole Church Speaks of Jesus (Mack Stiles)*
- *The Best-Kept Secret of Christian Mission (John Dickson)*
- *LiveGrowKnow: Your Life with Christ (DVD curriculum) (Rebecca Manley Pippert)*
- *Center Church (Tim Keller)*

Online

- *How to Create a Culture of Evangelism*
  gospelshapedchurch.org/resources291

LEADER'S REFLECTIONS

GOSPEL SHAPED

CHURCH

The complete series

LET THE POWER OF THE GOSPEL SHAPE FOUR OTHER CRITICAL AREAS IN THE LIFE OF YOUR CHURCH

GOSPEL SHAPED
WORSHIP

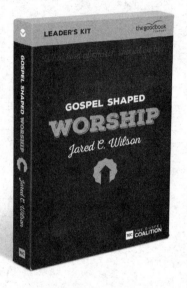

Christians are people who have discovered that the one true object of our worship is the God who has revealed himself in and through Jesus Christ.

But what exactly is worship? What should we be doing when we meet together for "church" on Sundays? And how does that connect with what we do the rest of the week?

This seven-week whole-church curriculum explores what it means to be a worshiping community. As we search the Scriptures together we will discover that true worship must encompass the whole of life. This engaging and flexible resource will challenge us to worship God every day of the week, with all our heart, mind, soul and strength.

Gospel Shaped Church is a new curriculum from The Gospel Coalition that will help whole congregations pause and think slowly, carefully and prayerfully about the kind of church they are called to be.

Written and presented by **JARED C. WILSON**
Jared is Director of Communications at Midwestern Seminary and College in Kansas City, and a prolific author. He is married to Becky and has two daughters.

WWW.GOSPELSHAPEDCHURCH.ORG/WORSHIP

"WE WANT CHURCHES CALLED INTO EXISTENCE BY THE GOSPEL TO BE SHAPED BY THE GOSPEL IN THEIR EVERYDAY LIFE."

DON CARSON AND TIM KELLER

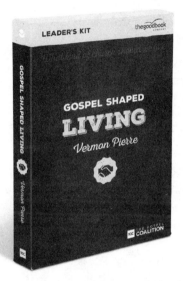

GOSPEL SHAPED
LIVING

Gospel Shaped Living is a track that explores over seven sessions what it means for a local church to be a distinctive counter-cultural community.

Through the gospel, God calls people from every nation, race and background to be joined together in a new family that shows his grace and glory. How should our lives as individuals and as a church reflect and model the new life we have found in Christ? And how different should we be to the world around us?

This challenging and interactive course will inspire us to celebrate grace and let the gospel shape our lives day by day.

Written and presented by **VERMON PIERRE**
Vermon is the Lead Pastor of Roosevelt Community Church in Phoenix, Arizona. He is married to Dennae and has three children. photo: Bradford Armstrong

WWW.GOSPELSHAPEDCHURCH.ORG/LIVING

GOSPEL SHAPED
WORK

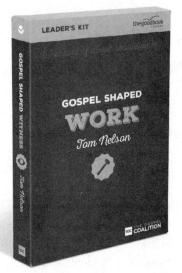

Many Christians experience a troubling disconnect between their everyday work and what they live and work for as a believer in Jesus. How should the gospel shape my view of life on an assembly line, or change my work as a teacher, artist, nurse, home-maker or gardener?

Gospel Shaped Work explores over eight sessions how the gospel changes the way we view our work in the world—and how a church should equip its members to serve God in their everyday vocations, and relate to the wider world of work and culture.

These engaging and practical sessions are designed to reveal the Bible's all-encompassing vision for our daily lives, and our engagement with culture as a redeemed community. It will provoke a fresh discussion in your church about how the gospel of Christ impacts every area of life in our world.

Written and presented by **TOM NELSON**
Tom is the Senior Pastor of Christ Community Church in Kansas City, and a council member of The Gospel Coalition. He is married to Liz and has two grown children.

WWW.GOSPELSHAPEDCHURCH.ORG/WORK

"THESE RESOURCES GIVE SPACE TO CONSIDER WHAT A GENUINE EXPRESSION OF A GOSPEL-SHAPED CHURCH LOOKS LIKE FOR YOU IN THE PLACE GOD HAS PUT YOU, AND WITH THE PEOPLE HE HAS GATHERED INTO FELLOWSHIP WITH YOU."

DON CARSON AND TIM KELLER

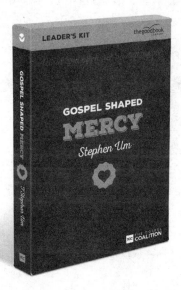

GOSPEL SHAPED
MERCY

The gospel is all about justice and mercy: the just punishment of God falling on his Son, Jesus, so that he can have mercy on me, a sinner.

But many churches have avoided following through on the Bible's clear teaching on working for justice and mercy in the wider world. They fear that it is a distraction from the primary task of gospel preaching.

This *Gospel Shaped Mercy* module explores how individual Christians and whole churches can and should be engaged in the relief of poverty, hunger and injustice in a way that adorns the gospel of grace.

Written and presented by **STEPHEN UM**
Stephen is Senior Minister of Citylife Church in Boston, MA, and is a council member of The Gospel Coalition.

WWW.GOSPELSHAPEDCHURCH.ORG/MERCY

MORE RESOURCES
TO TRANSFORM YOUR
OUTREACH

LIVE | GROW | KNOW

Live with Christ, Grow in Christ, Know more of Christ.

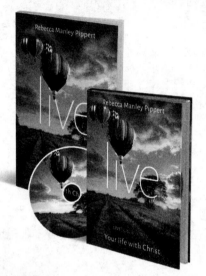

LiveGrowKnow is a new series from renowned speaker Rebecca Manley Pippert, designed to help people continue their journey from enquirer to disciple to mature believer.

Part One, *Live*, consists of five DVD-based sessions and is the perfect follow-up to an evangelistic course or event, or for anyone who wants to explore the Christian life more deeply.

REBECCA MANLEY PIPPERT
International speaker and author of *Out of the Saltshaker*

Becky Pippert's lifetime of experience in evangelism shines through on each page of these six Bible studies. They are written for a Christian to use with a group of interested non-Christians, helping them to meet the real Jesus.

This resource has been extensively used in many contexts and on every continent, and includes the Bible text. Whoever you are, it makes sharing faith with your friends simple: all you need is a cup of coffee* and a copy of *Uncovering the Life of Jesus* for each person.

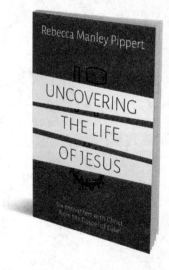

*Coffee optional.

Christianity E✝PLORED

Christianity Explored is a relaxed and informal way of introducing people to Jesus and is also great for anyone wanting to brush up on the basics of the Christian faith. Journey through the Gospel of Mark over seven weeks exploring the identity, mission and call of Jesus. The award-winning DVD, presented by Rico Tice, has subtitles in 14 languages and is also available to download by episode.

RICO TICE
Global evangelist and founder of
Christianity Explored Ministries

Most of us find evangelism hard, but there is no greater joy than seeing people come to Christ Jesus. This realistic yet hope-filled book will help prepare and encourage you to be honest and bold in your evangelism, presenting the gospel fully and properly, even when it's tough.

WWW.THEGOODBOOK.COM

thegoodbook
COMPANY

Opening up the Bible

At The Good Book Company, we are dedicated to helping Christians and local churches grow. We believe that God's growth process always starts with hearing clearly what he has said to us through his timeless word—the Bible.

Ever since we opened our doors in 1991, we have been striving to produce resources that honor God in the way the Bible is used. We have grown to become an international provider of user-friendly resources to the Christian community, with believers of all backgrounds and denominations using our Bible studies, books, evangelistic resources, DVD-based courses and training events.

We want to equip ordinary Christians to live for Christ day by day, and churches to grow in their knowledge of God, their love for one another, and the effectiveness of their outreach.

Call us for a discussion of your needs or visit one of our local websites for more information on the resources and services we provide.

North America: www.thegoodbook.com
UK & Europe: www.thegoodbook.co.uk
Australia: www.thegoodbook.com.au
New Zealand: www.thegoodbook.co.nz

North America: 866 244 2165
UK & Europe: 0333 123 0880
Australia: (02) 6100 4211
New Zealand (+64) 3 343 1990